How To Thrive as Your Most
Vibrant, Weird, and Real Self

That's
Bold
of You

CASE KENNY

About The Author

Case Kenny is an entrepreneur, mindfulness leader, host and founder of the top 25 podcast *New Mindset, Who Dis* on both Apple Podcasts and Spotify. Beloved by some of today's biggest celebrities including Hailey Bieber, Sophia Bush, and Lucy Hale, Viola Davis and featured on Good Morning America, you might recognize him from his viral coffee cup and post-it quotes on Instagram, which have been shared by millions and featured by Forbes, Fortune Magazine, Complex, Women's Health, Cosmopolitan and many more.

Created in 2018, Kenny's podcast *New Mindset, Who Dis* features his short, no BS take on all things mindfulness in a relatable way - empowering people to be happier and live more fulfilling lives by changing their mindsets in all areas of life spanning from self-worth and empowerment to dating and relationships, career advice, and more.

Kenny also produces special "music x mindfulness" episodes where he collaborates with top artists and DJs including Martin Garrix, Gryffin, Cheat Codes, Sam Feldt, and others to bring mindfulness to life in an energizing and unique way for listeners. He is also the creator and host of the popular dance music x mindfulness show, *Zen Disco*.

For the latest, follow Case on Instagram @case.kenny.

Also by Case Kenny:

Single Is Your Superpower

But First, Inner Peace

The New Mindset Journal

The Unbothered Journal

Note: The best companion to *That's Bold of You* is therapy. I wrote this book to be a wildly optimistic celebration of who you are while also encouraging you to challenge and be accountable to yourself. While I fully believe in the life-changing power of practical and relatable mindfulness, nothing can take the place of a trained and licensed mental health professional. I hope my perspective gives you plenty of healthy and mindful reasons to praise the glowing, vibrant, and bold aspects of yourself and to accept and grow through your imperfections - but also pushes you to take the next step with a professional. See you at therapy.

- Case

Table Of Contents

PART I: UNLEARNING

PART II: BREAKING PATTERNS

PART III: NO GOING BACK

CHAPTER FOURTEEN: Comparison, the Thief of Joy
Part 1. Instagram Vs. Reality
Part 2. Perpetual People Pleasers
Part 3. Table for One, Please

CHAPTER FIFTEEN: Got Standards?
Part 1. Picky or Selective?
Part 2. ROI, Baby
Part 3. What Are the Odds?

CHAPTER SIXTEEN: Imposter, Who?
Part 1. Feelin' Cute, Won't Delete Later
Part 2. Unqualified Is a State of Mind
Part 3. Facts VS. Feelings

CHAPTER SEVENTEEN: Reintroduce Yourself
Part 1. Take Your Own Advice
Part 2. Take a Step Back
Part 3. You're the Kind of Person Who…

CHAPTER EIGHTEEN: You VS. the World
Part 1. How You See the World…
Part 2. There Are No Coincidences
Part 3. 20/20 Vision
Part 4. Strength in Loneliness
Part 5. That's Bold of You

BOLD (*adjective*): fearless in embracing your honesty; refusing to allow society's labels to define your worth; empowered by imperfection, simplicity, and forgiveness.

To be bold is to question who you've been told to be, pressure to conform, and the timelines expected of you.

To be bold is to recognize you have work to do, but you're still worthy of love, fulfillment, and rewarding experiences.

To be bold is to find peace in being "lost in the right direction."

To be bold is to dismiss the labels society wants you to define yourself by - *too sensitive, too honest, too quiet, too energetic, too intimidating, too ambitious, too independent, too loud, too difficult...*

To be bold is to decide you're exactly who you're supposed to be.

That's bold of you to…

- embrace being imperfect
- change your mind about what you want
- ask for a raise
- be an unapologetic outfit repeater
- say NO and mean it
- make the first move or care first
- introduce yourself first
- be OK with waiting for what you deserve
- reinvent yourself… again
- say HI to every dog you see
- believe in positive intent and goodness
- speak your mind freely
- take a compliment at face value
- double text
- call someone (the horror!) instead of texting
- be too loud or too quiet and be okay with it
- be upfront about what you want
- embrace both your masculine AND feminine side
- go to dinner alone
- change your mind… again
- unfollow anyone who makes you feel less
- love your body as it is today
- determine your own timeline for having a family
- stand up for yourself without saying "sorry"
- stop asking for permission
- decide their labels don't define you
- show others how you expect to be treated
- make eye contact first
- book a solo trip
- decide you're worthy of being loved completely
- tell someone exactly how you feel
- remove "good enough" from your vocabulary
- decide your past doesn't dictate your future

Is This It?!

****

The rumors are true… You're the total package.

You're hot, smart, spicy, brilliant, poetic, rule-breaking, sophisticated, independent, glowing, compassionate, and ambitious.

There's nothing you can't do.

So often in life, we let our insecurities, fears, a strong desire to please, and pressure to conform get in the way of letting our uniqueness and its expression truly shine. We let them hold us back in relationships, too, whether out of fear from revealing our true selves or our true feelings.

And why, in 99.9% of cases, are we willing to dull our true selves and true desires? Because we don't want to be called "crazy," "too much," or "extra."

Labels like that have become all too commonplace, liberally employed when judging and describing anyone who may think, speak, or act in ways that differ from the norm (whatever *that* is). The result? We ALL hold back. We keep our real self hidden, not letting it evolve and blossom. And the most vibrant, creative, and playful among us? We hold back far too often... even if our weird energy does leak out from time to time. And that's a real shame.

Who you are shouldn't
be in a hiding place, but
rather in a finding place.

When you sweep all the small stuff aside, there truly is no greater victory in life than becoming yourself - the fiery, intelligent, driven, curious, intense, and caring person you are. That uniqueness is your superpower, and it's what drives the right people, the right job, and the right opportunities to you. That uniqueness should be your guiding star.

I wrote this book to help you peel back the layers and become your boldest self.

Who am I? You might know me from my podcast, *New Mindset, Who Dis*. You might recognize my quotes that make the rounds on social media, or you might have no idea who I am. I'm a 34-year old guy who lives and works in Chicago.

I jokingly say that I "share my feelings for a living." I say that because there's really no singular term for what I do professionally - I write, research, speak, doodle, create, produce music, and share my enthusiasm and passion for better understanding and simplifying the complexities that arise from human emotions.

Today, I'm a speaker, podcaster, and writer, but that certainly hasn't always been the case. I had a 12-year corporate stint in advertising and sales where I thickened my skin to hearing and reacting to "NO." It was during this time that I was introduced to the magical word that changed my life:

Mindfulness.

It's a word that means different things to different people. To some, it's a deeply esoteric term which describes energies, frequencies, or aligning chakras. To others, it conjures up visions of silent meditations, sound baths, or similar rituals. To me, the term describes my now decade-long pursuit of practical self-awareness.

I've never had a huge ego, but while in my 20s, I learned an important truth: I'm good at some things and not so good at others. I'm not a great swimmer. I'm not great with numbers. I'm stubborn as a mule, and patience is not one of my strong suits. But one thing I am good at – maybe even *great* at? Understanding and simplifying my emotional response to life's stressors and challenges. While I'm just as prone as anyone to overthink or feel anxious, I am great at learning how to identify the root of those feelings, manage them, and return to a place of truth.

That's a truth that challenges me to ask: "Case, is this a fact or a feeling? Case, is this who you really are or is this just a temporary feeling?"

I know this is a skill that may come easier to some people than others, but I believe it can be taught and strengthened with practice. And it's what mindfulness is all about. I initially started my podcast as a challenge to myself - no guests, no commentary on culture, sports, or current events - just time spent pushing myself to identify and answer some of life's tough questions:

"Case, why do you feel anxious?"
"Case, what are you afraid to do?"
"Case, what are you drawn to in life?"
"Case, who are you really?"

In short episodes, I would work my way through complex life topics and challenge myself to get real about how I actually felt - not how I thought I should feel or thought I needed to feel, but rather how I actually felt. It wasn't long before I realized what I was really doing. I was practicing mindfulness. I was experimenting in the art of self-awareness, which at its core means exploring one of the most powerfully honest questions: *WHY*.

When you become adept at asking WHY, the impact will permeate every area of your personal and professional life. When my podcast blew up, I quit my day job and started devoting myself to the search for my WHY, full-time. I spoke to thousands of interesting people, many being listeners from the show. I learned they were also struggling with WHY. I wrote a couple books outlining my learnings and perspective, and continued to pursue, explore, and share what I've personally found to be so meaningful and impactful.

It's humbling and gratifying that so many people listen to my perspective on my podcast, and that media programs and outlets like *Good Morning America, Fortune, Forbes, ABC,* or *Complex* have since asked me to share my thoughts on life, relationships, and mindfulness. But as much as my life changed over the past decade with this new knowledge, I still chuckle when people refer to me as a mindfulness, dating, or relationship coach or expert.

I prefer to think of myself as someone who simply has come to learn, celebrate, and share his truth and who is passionate about helping others explore theirs.

This book is essentially the print form of everything I've learned and everything I do. It challenges you, the reader, to stand in front of a mirror and ask yourself: "WHO am I?" WHAT are the parts of me that I keep hidden? WHY am I watering myself down? WHY am I hiding the best, unique, and boldest parts of who I am?"

… and then to think about how you might live life differently.

This book is about mindfully peeling back the layers of your sense of self and revealing the most glowing, radiant part of you that perhaps you've been scared to look at or felt tempted to call "too much." This book is about the labels we've given ourselves or the ones we're afraid society will give to us if we show our true, glowing, compassionate, eager, bold, and honest selves.

This book is about letting go of labels and the insecurities that surround them and embracing boldness instead. After reading it, I hope you'll find yourself saying:

I'm no longer worried about being "too much." Instead, I'm proud of everything I bring to the table.

History is filled with examples of people who ALMOST let a label talk them out of their life's intended path. What a shame that would have been!

The queen of talk show television, Oprah Winfrey, was told early on that she was "too emotional" in her reporting style. Had she bought into that label, where would she be today?

Famed author, Stephen King, was allegedly so critical of his writing style that he literally threw out the draft of his debut novel *Carrie*. His wife found it and encouraged him to embrace his talent and see what happened. Had he dimmed his light and left his work unfinished, the subsequent 4 million copies of that book never would have sold.

John Steinbeck, too, doubted his talent and once wrote, "I am not a writer. I've been fooling myself and other people." He then went on to write *The Grapes of Wrath*. High school English class would have looked a lot different if he had accepted his imposter syndrome.

Actress Natalie Portman almost let her insecurity hold her back from seriously pursuing her acting career. "I'm still insecure about my own worthiness. I have to remind myself today, you are here for a reason," she once remarked in a Harvard commencement speech. "Sometimes your insecurities and your inexperience may lead you to embrace other people's expectations, standards, or values, but you can harness that inexperience to carve out your own path..." [1] Her story would have taken a very different turn if she hid behind that insecurity and taken a more traditional path.

Like so many others who have challenged themselves to do the same, this book is about asking yourself *WHY* you've been hiding your "extra," your "good crazy," your "too much" - the part of you that speaks loudly and clearly to your uniqueness and your willingness to express it in all its forms. It's the source of your self-esteem, your individuality, your standards, your creativity, and what speaks to you on a deep level. It's the lens through which you look at life, your goals and who you are, and it's time to reclaim its power by asking yourself that nagging, powerful, and pervasive question: WHY?

This book will likely be placed in the "self-help" section of any bookstore, but we're going beyond self-help...

This is mindfulness in its most simple and practical form. I'm going to show you how, if you do the work, embracing "too much" can radically improve your life.

I'm going to show you how to go from borrowing, mirroring, or settling for the truths, aspirations, judgments, and goals of others to stepping into and embracing those which are truly your own. Trust me, there is no substitute for the joy and empowerment that comes from unearthing the real YOU. As author George Elliot once said, "It's never too late to be the person you could have been."

So, start by asking yourself: "WHY are you reading this book?" Is it because you feel confused or lost? Is it because you've been reflecting and questioning your approach to life and wondering, "Is this it?!" Is it because you're trying to heal from something that has threatened your inner peace? Is it because you feel unsatisfied? Restless? Misunderstood? Is it because you feel you have something unseen that you want to express? Talent, art, music, humor?

Or maybe it's because you've found yourself living in the "gray" of life? That's where life isn't necessarily bad, but it's not what you imagined or hoped it would be.

Perhaps you have many things you're grateful for and you're "doing your thing," e.g., job, friends, interests, etc., but you've realized you're not really doing YOUR thing?

Perhaps you've borrowed expectations from people who told you to be "realistic?" Or you've taken a timeline for love from your parents, rom coms, or social media? Or you've defined success based on the latest *Forbes* article? Or you've defined happiness based on the latest viral inspirational quote?

Regardless of the reason, you're feeling unsettled, that something is missing, or that all you've been led to believe is worthy and purposeful is not working for you.

It's time to step away from what you've been told, the judgments, and labels you're afraid you'll be given. Let's take some time to explore what else might be under those doubts and fears… what you would truly do if they disappeared tomorrow. It's time to say goodbye to "sorry," the need to conform and fit in, and instead, emphatically embrace YOUR thoughts, ideas, desires, and all that makes you who YOU are.

It's time to explore the parts of yourself you've hidden pieces of or buried in favor of what's expected of you or what you've been convinced is "normal" or aspirational. That's the truth you've let sit dormant in favor of not ruffling feathers or drawing undue attention. That's the truth you've replaced with someone else's, perhaps your parents' or the internet's… the truth you've hidden or not let evolve for the fear of a label.

This book is about reclaiming your sense of self. It's about refusing to look back and regret the words you didn't say and the things you didn't try. We're going to explore how important it is to lean into the power of our memories and observation.

"I have seen A, and therefore, I believe B to be true."

"I have experienced C, and therefore, I have this standard D."

Observation… life through the lens of experience. Or what I call "practical mindfulness."

We're going to spend some time making sense of our memories and asking ourselves WHY … and then we're going to lean forward and start living our best lives built on the foundation of being "too much."

Let's get a bit weird. A bit too much. A bit extra. Let's get bold.

I promise, if you do the work, you'll find that being "too much" is the most liberating thing you can do. It might not immediately align the stars for you, and you might still feel lost in life at times (as we all do), but you'll be at peace because you know you're lost in the right direction.

Let's start by diving into my least favorite word in the world: "crazy."

PART I: UNLEARNING

To embrace our most vibrant, weird, and real selves we must unlearn assumptions, desires, and conditioning. We must reinvent aspects of ourselves, our expectations of what is possible, and the lens through which we look at life.

This chapter examines several mindsets to help you rethink the labels you've been living by and embrace more optimistic and empowering ones in the process:

~~I'm "too much"~~

~~My vulnerability is NOT attractive~~

~~My ego is my enemy~~

~~I need more and better in order to be happy~~

~~I need to have a gameplan for my life~~

~~I lack too much to be happy~~

CHAPTER ONE

Cute, But "Crazy"

****

If you're reading this, you're gorgeous,
but not only on the outside.

You're gorgeous for the way you see life,
for your curiosity, for your depth,
and for the way your smile
lights up those around you.

You have something special to offer
the world, so please don't forget it.

Part 1. Being "Too Much"

"I don't want to seem crazy." Sound familiar? Maybe you've been called crazy for caring too much, crazy for having high expectations for yourself and others, crazy for dreaming big, or crazy for how you dress, your interests, or your passions.

Have you ever been called too "much?" Too "extra?" Too "type A?" Too much of a "main character?" Too "intimidating?" Too "sensitive?" Too "emotional?" Maybe you've been told to "chill, calm down," and "be realistic?" Or you've been asked, "Who do you think you are?" Or, "What makes YOU so special?"

Or maybe, when reflecting… you've labeled yourself in the same way? Maybe behind closed doors, you've felt you care too much or felt that what you think, say, do, or want is over-the-top. Maybe as a result, you've become a perpetual "people-pleaser," and the most common word out of your mouth is "sorry."

The word "crazy" itself is sure to be triggering to some people… and rightfully so. It's not the appropriate word. It can be offensive to some people, and across the board, it's totally over-used. The world is an uglier place because of comparison, but society loves a good label. And so, here we are conditioned to resort to applying the timeworn cliche of "crazy" in any instance where we've deemed ourselves to be too _____. Fill in the blank with any word that makes you stand out, break a pattern, or not deliver an expected outcome or norm.

Let's reframe this word "crazy" and the connotation behind it. Contrary to how we've been conditioned to view ourselves and those who stand out or are different as being "crazy," I think embracing your unusual quirks and passions can be a good thing.

In fact, I think it can be an amazing thing. It can be the most positive and amazing quality you can bring to your relationships and to the world. Being "crazy" is a true reflection of YOU and your uniqueness. It's a true reflection that YOU are a living, breathing, inspired human who listens to your inner voice and embraces what it tells you.

This book is a call to embrace the compassionate and truthful part of you that you've deemed is "crazy"- the part of you that is your uniqueness and who you are. It's what makes you different. It's the source of your wholeness, your self-esteem, and your standards.

For the rest of the book, I'm going to reframe "crazy" as being "too much," and to be "too much" is to be bold. That's being "too much" in any sense that breaks a pattern or makes you stand out. It's not necessarily a reflection of being boisterous, too energetic, or too needy. "Too much" can encompass any end of the spectrum - big or small, loud or quiet, etc. It's simply a reflection of different or outside expectations.

Too sensitive...
Too honest...
Too quiet...
Too energetic...
Too intimidating...
Too driven...
Too independent...
Too loud...
Too difficult...

When you're being "too much," you're actually being the truest version of yourself – without superficial filters or need for conformity. Being "too much" is leaning into what makes you feel most alive, honest, and real.

When you're being "too much," you're finally honoring what you REALLY think, how you REALLY feel, what you REALLY want to express, and what you REALLY want to do with your life.

Why have we been conditioned to think that being "too much" is crazy? Why have we been conditioned to think being honest and open is anything but positive? Why do we think being bold is a bad thing?

Life is so much simpler when you stop listening to people who tell you to be "realistic."

Of course, words and actions that are outside the realm of social, moral, and lawful parameters would not simply be "too much."

Let's move past the social mentality of always trying to appear cool, realistic, in control, nonchalant, or carefree. Who exactly does that serve? It definitely doesn't serve you - to numb yourself to how you feel, to water down what you want to say or do. And it certainly doesn't serve the people around you - does the world really need more "too cool for school" people or people living half-truths?

You are a living, breathing human with unique perspectives, values, emotions, and worldviews... and there's nothing to overthink, doubt, hold back, or keep hidden about that.

I'm not talking about being "too much" where you create or seek drama. I'm not talking about demanding your partner's social media passwords, showing up uninvited to someone's residence or job, or dealing with someone or something in a mentally unhealthy, unsavory, or morally disreputable way. I'm not talking about being "too much" that comes from insecurity, immaturity, or mental or emotional instability. There are, of course, many qualifiers for what is good "too much" and what is immature, bad, or unaware "too much."

This book is about celebrating the former and while the following chapters will examine aspects of good vs. bad "too much," I'd encourage you to join me in therapy to unpack the latter.

I'm talking about embracing being emotionally "too much" in a healthy way that shows you're in the driver's seat of your life. I'm talking about rebranding being "too much" as a good thing. A great thing.

It's "too much" to care deeply about your ideas and needs and those of others. It's "too much" to share your emotionally healthy thoughts, desires, actions, and goals - as different as they may be. It's "too much" to expect respect, communication, and honesty from others, and if it's not given, it's "too much" to do something about it.

It's "too much" to cut ties with someone who is dishonest, insincere, dishonorable, disrespectful, or who plays games with you. It's "too much" to be over-the-top excited about what inspires you in life. It's "too much" to ask for 100% if you're not satisfied with the 50%.

Being "too much" is your life spark. Maybe you've heard the idea of returning to your "inner child" or phrases like "your most radical true self?"

We're all capable of being "too much," but unfortunately, in some form or another, we've talked ourselves out of embracing it fully. In some way, we've turned off our capacity to be "too much" in the face of pressure or out of fear of potential judgment - both from ourselves and others.

This book is about exploring how we can all benefit from finding and honoring our "too much" instead of doubting or hiding it. This book is about staying true to yourself and knowing which feelings are real and which are not.

It's not about being outrageously loud or unfiltered in an unhealthy or unexamined way. It's about learning what is truly you and what is not.

What would life look like if you spoke what you truly believed? Dressed in a way that was authentic to you? Shot your shot more often? Built standards and boundaries out of immovable stone? Stood up for what you believed? Stopped apologizing?

What would change if you prioritized how your life feels to you instead of how it looks to others?

I'm willing to bet it'd be a dramatic 180 from how you've been living - pressured to quiet your true inner self and instead, constantly shrinking yourself and watering yourself down.

What would life look like if you embraced being "too much?"

Part 2. If You Don't Use It...

In so many areas of life, we've been conditioned, pressured, and guilted into thinking any emotion that isn't deemed "cool" or "casual" makes us seem "crazy" or "too much."

Especially in dating... I don't exactly know what the deal with dating is anymore, but it seems to have become a race to the bottom of who can be the most nonchalant or appear to care the least. It's become a game of chicken - whoever cares more first or whoever lets their "crazy" show first loses.

What is that all about? You're "too much" if you develop a connection faster than the other person... You're "too much" if you read into what someone says or does.... You're "too much" for getting attached too easily... You're "too much" for wanting and expecting clear communication and intention... And so, the reaction has been to bury your individuality, your inner voice, and your realness in favor of appearing chill and cool.

This also happens in your career and your personal life if you're afraid of being fully seen or coming across as "too _____."

"Who do I think I am to be posting this selfie?!"

"Who am I to start a podcast?!"

"I can't ask for a raise! That's too much."

"I don't want to seem desperate by making the first move."

"I'll just smile and nod otherwise I come across as intimidating."

Sound familiar? Without noticing, life has slowly but surely led us to an ambiguous limbo stage where we're constantly questioning or quieting our internal voice and our intuition so as to not be different or ruffle any feathers.

We think being "too much" is a negative label. We stay quiet so we're not labeled as the loud or different one. We do things we don't really want to do so we're not labeled as a loner or the *odd man out*. We borrow other people's timelines so we're not labeled as falling behind. We don't speak our desires, expectations, or intentions early and often so as to not "scare" someone off. And I think worst of all, we borrow and internalize the definitions of others as to what is acceptable, good or bad, success, failure, happiness, etc.

We ignore our calling to be "too much" and voila, here we are - living in the "gray" of life - just going along with the flow, hoping we'll end up where we're supposed to be, with the people we're supposed to be with, doing the things we're supposed to do.

Ouch. That's a pretty scathing review, but I want to start our journey off together by showing the present state of mind so many are in and how much room we have to improve. Being "too much" in the way I'm referring to is a good thing. It shows that you're alive, that you care, that you're willing to be hurt, and that you're willing to try.

Passion. Fearlessness. Personality. Since when are those things to keep hidden?

If you think you're being "too much" in a negative way because you're more emotional than others, more attached, more different, more of an overthinker, more expressive, more driven or independent, more divergent... just how does that make you "too much?" A listener of my podcast once told me the following and it's been in my head ever since...

Lightning in a bottle should never be taken for granted.

I'm sure we'd all agree that life is about going after what you want, right? You go after the job you want?

The house you want? The clothes you want? The body you want? Things. Stuff. Accolades.

That's admirable when it works. People respect and applaud a promotion. People respect and applaud entrepreneurs, talented creators, entertainers, and people who are purposeful and often leave a mark in the world. People respect people who make bold moves, shoot their shots, and speak openly and honestly with passion in their eyes.

So, then why when it comes to matters of the heart - relationships, passions, purpose, your voice - do we suddenly shrink? Why is it suddenly NOT cool for you to go after what you want honestly and with enthusiasm?

Here's what I've come to embrace, and I'm excited to show you WHY and HOW to live your own version of this mindset...

Going after what you want in your dating life does NOT make you thirsty or desperate. Pursuing music, art, or passion as a beginner does NOT make you "too much" in a negative sense. Setting an insanely ambitious goal does NOT make you "too much" in a negative sense. Standing up for yourself does NOT make you "too much" in a negative sense. Having an eager sense of attachment or excitement in life does NOT make you "too much" in a negative sense.

We feel what we feel for a reason. We're inspired for a reason. We're excitable for a reason. Ignoring those feelings is only doing you a disservice and frankly, it's exhausting!

What a tiring and frustrating way to go about life - feeling your honesty, but choosing something entirely different, knowing you deserve 100% but settling for 50% out of fear. Feeling but never acting...

We do this out of fear of imaginary judgment and the result is, as stated by Seneca, the Roman philosopher: "We suffer more in imagination than in reality."

Ask yourself this question: Can you imagine if you rarely or never felt anything at all in life? Can you imagine if you dated and literally felt nothing? Or if you had zero internal guidance for what made you excited in life? No emotion? Nothing to go off of? You'd be so frustrated!

"Bueller? Hello? Am I alive?"

Maybe you've felt this way before? Maybe you've gone through times where nothing or no one spoke to you at a level that made sense. Maybe you can relate to the idea of living in the gray of life - feeling okay, but totally numb and disconnected from your true self. Those feelings of disconnection make the times where you actually DO feel something that much more valuable, and it's crucial we listen to them.

Your inner thoughts and feelings need to be respected, acted on, and communicated. It's not "crazy!" It's not "too much" in the way we've been conditioned to judge ourselves. Keeping quiet, playing chill and cool, ignoring what lights you up... that's NOT the answer anymore.

It's OK if that's the path you've been walking down to get to this point in your life, but no more. We're going to embrace being "too much." And we're going to do it practically and in the real world - not in the land of butterflies and rainbows or just in our imagination.

Of course, be a respectful human being. Read the room. Don't become someone who makes demands of others or is a Stage-5 clinger. But, from this point forward, we're not going to be afraid to be "too much," and we're no longer using the word "crazy" as a label to talk ourselves out of being honest and free.

The following chapters are about how to practically find and come home to yourself. They're about compassionately reconditioning yourself - drawing a line in the sand and affirming that to ignore your calling to be "too much" is to choose a path that is NOT true to you.

The more you ignore your calling to be "too much"... well, I think the saying is: "If you don't use it, you lose it."

If you never listen to how you really feel and if you never allow yourself to feel, to get attached, to care, to want more, to be a beginner again, to be loud and outrageous or quiet and reflective... then you're never being fully true to yourself. And if that's the case, how do you really know what's true for YOU? How do you know what YOU really want? How do you really know what YOU deserve?

... not what your parents told you you should want.

... not what your ex told you you should want.

... not what your friends, your boss, or random internet strangers tell you you should want.

YOU. What do YOU want? You can't know the answer to that question if you ignore your inner feelings and reject being "too much." It's time to honor and respect being "too much" for the very practical reason that it'll show you if what you're doing and how you're living is true to YOU.

Coming home to being "too much" is a cold drink on a hot day. It's lying on the beach after a long run. When you embrace your deepest honesty, you'll find yourself saying: "Wow, I needed that. Let's do this thing. I'm ready." Coming home to being "too much" shows you the path that lies ahead for YOU. Because it's YOUR path. Because YOU decided it's your path.

Leaning into your honesty is a one-way ticket out of the "gray" in your life, turning it into a proverbial rainbow of colors that speaks loud and true to who you are.

If that makes you "crazy," then I'm "crazy" too. I guess we're all "crazy" together. But I would choose being "crazy" over being indifferent and watered down any day. I would rather blurt out something embarrassing than never speak how I feel. I would rather triple text than never text at all.

You're only "too much" for people who aren't enough for you.

This book is an exploration of being "too much." It's a journey to help you find your own version of "too muchness" after perhaps burying some or most of it long ago or to create it from scratch if you need to!

So perhaps you've been numb for too long, you've allowed yourself to be walked and talked over by others, you haven't spoken up, or you haven't gone after what and who you really want because you've bottled up your truth in favor of what is quieter, easier, and more comfortable. That's about to change.

In my years of podcasting and sharing my belief in and passion for mindfulness, I've had conversations with a countless number of people and I've heard heartbreaking and heartwarming stories of growth, failure, rejection, relationships, love, work, career, and life. What I've found is that, over time, so often people simply give up on their expectations of what is possible. They become passive. They adopt an "it is what it is" mentality. A defeatist mentality.

"What's the point of trying? Of dreaming? Of doing something different or new? What's the point of being excited if I'm just gonna be hurt? What's the point of starting a new project if I'm just gonna fail?"

Embracing being "too much" is the contrast you need to this "it is what it is" mentality.

Over the years, listeners of my podcast have shared with me countless stories of embracing being "too much" and the redemption that followed - stories of looking rejection, failure, frustration, and self-doubt in the eye and refusing to accept their permanence.

In the face of rejection... one listener told me she applied to a certain dream job 22 times (yes, really 22 times) and heard NO 22 times. She almost gave up and accepted working in a field she didn't want, but she found the strength to apply one more time and she finally got the job (and now she jumps out of planes for a living).

In the face of a draining relationship... another listener told me she invested six years in an unhappy marriage and was on the verge of just accepting that version of life, but she decided to leave and restart her life. Fast forward two years and she's now in a happy relationship, getting her PHD, has stable finances, and is the happiest she's ever been.

In the face of self-doubt... another listener described her toxic home life growing up and how she was constantly told she was worthless and different. Add to the mix challenges with her weight, an eating disorder, and feeling unlovable, she lived a life where she made herself feel small to accommodate everyone else's needs - clinging to any shred of love given to her. With the help of therapy, on her 30th birthday, she finally decided to fight for what she felt she deserved in life- she stopped letting her past dictate her worth, left her hometown, is now traveling across Europe and Asia, and in her own words is "reintroducing herself to the world."

When you embrace being "too much," you find the missing pep in your step. You react to life around you in a way that's true to you. You tell someone you love them because you love them. You start a new project simply because it excites you. You go to a movie alone because you want to see it. You learn to be open to find and listen to your deep, inner voice and confidently act on it.

Most of all, when you embrace being "too much," you make the most of the second chances you give yourself. That's a second chance to find your truest level of honesty and put it back in the driver's seat.

If you don't use it…

Part 3. *Wabi-Sabi*

This idea of embracing being "too much" is predicated on understanding that your realest self is undoubtedly flawed, imperfect, and always changing. To be "too much" is not to be so confident in yourself that you assume everyone else is wrong, you're the sh*t, and the world revolves around you. In fact, it's quite the opposite.

To be bold is to humble yourself. To be bold is to embrace your intuition and what speaks to you on a deep level - even if what it tells you changes as you grow. It's to tune out the noise and reinvent yourself in the face of pressure to remain the same or become something that is not authentic to you. To be bold is to be imperfect. To be bold is to surrender to the ebb and flow of life - both inside and out. To be bold is to embrace being imperfect and incomplete.

To be bold is to embrace the Japanese concept of *wabi-sabi*. This is a philosophical tradition that encourages the appreciation of imperfection and impermanence in nature and design. It originates from a folk story that says, "A young man was asked to tend to a master's garden. He worked carefully sweeping and raking the garden until it was orderly and just perfect. Before showing the garden to his master, he shook a cherry tree, letting a few petals float randomly to the ground. Now the garden was beautiful." [1]

Wabi-sabi is a combination of two concepts which revere beauty in imperfect and impermanent forms. *Wabi* pays respect to simplicity and imperfection. In design, it respects asymmetry, imbalance, or uneven visuals of an item. *Sabi* represents beauty and aging, and encourages us to look beneath the surface and beyond brokenness. *Sabi* reminds us that wear and tear is beautiful and that with each passing day, ourselves, nature, and objects are never the same. In design, it pays respect to the aging of material and aged presentation. [2]

**_Wabi_ - there is beauty in imperfection.
Sabi - time and aging are gifts.**

You can observe the concept of _wabi-sabi_ all around you.
You might see it in the chip in a drinking glass. Or in the
imperfect or uneven design of a vase or bowl. Or the uneven
edges of a round cookie. Or the torn edges of an otherwise
perfect poster. Or the uneven paint texture or paint strokes
on a painting. Or the uneven lean of a tree. Or the rusted
surface of an old metal part.

One of the oldest presentations of _wabi-sabi_ is known as
kintsugi or "golden scars." This is the practice of filling cracks
with gold fillings. You might have seen this in the example of
a broken bowl that was put back together and mended with
gold in the cracks. Per the philosophy, the imperfect cracks
are considered beautiful and are the perfect representation of
wabi-sabi - the bowl is now even more beautiful because the
cracks aren't hidden and the gold fillings bring out the beauty
of that imperfection. [3]

In the day and age of social media, I'd say the trend on
TikTok of people embracing their flaws and being real could
be a reflection of the _wabi-sabi_ philosophy. Compare that to
the "perfection" and curation of Instagram where everyone is
flexing and bragging about their seeming lack of flaws, it
seems to be the platform for embracing embarrassment,
flaws, and missteps.

Wabi-sabi recognizes beauty in simplicity, imperfection, and
aging. It recognizes that beauty isn't only on the surface and
encourages us to look beyond our first glance or first
perception. In her book _Wabi Sabi,_ Beth Kempton describes
the philosophy as follows: "Put simply, _wabi-sabi_ gives you
permission to be yourself.

It encourages you to do your best but not make yourself ill in
pursuit of an unattainable goal of perfection. It gently
motions you to relax, slow down, and enjoy your life.

And it shows you that beauty can be found in the most unlikely of places, making every day a doorway to delight." [4]

To be bold, we must embrace the concept of *wabi-sabi* because without finding peace in imperfection, we'll always be fighting ourselves and our boldness will not be true boldness. It will be built on a foundation that doesn't pay respect to flaws and doesn't see them as a source of power. That kind of boldness is not what this book is about. Boldness that is a distraction from your true self, your imperfections, and your impermanence... is not true boldness. Superficial or forced boldness is not true boldness.

True boldness is to find acceptance in your own imperfections and unique timeline and recognize that those things are all connected in some way. An imperfect day, an imperfect experience, or an imperfect reaction to life around us - it's all connected in a larger way, and the sooner we pay respect to that journey, the sooner our boldness is real and unforced.

Being your own version of "too much" is built on the concept of surrender and stillness. That's surrender to the reality of your life - your past, present, and future. That's surrender to your upbringing, the things you've been told to be or do, and the expectations handed to you. It's a compassionate surrender and acceptance of that reality, and it's paying reverence to the imperfection life has bestowed upon you to this point. True boldness comes from surrendering to that reality because YOU get to decide what comes next. You get to decide to make the best of where you are today.

Do you see beauty in your imperfect journey? Do you look beneath the surface for truth? Do you embrace the grace of aging and momentum? Do you question perception?

Wabi-sabi describes boldness in its most true and authentic form by acknowledging that you are always changing. Your boldness doesn't come from being so certain in yourself and your direction, it comes from knowing that change is what delivers what you're looking for. It acknowledges the idea of impermanence and that there is no definition of being "complete" in life.

**To be bold is not to strive to
be perfect, but to be whole.**

When I think of being bold, I think of being whole. Not perfect. Not certain. Not 100%. To be bold is to be whole in acceptance of your ever-changing self and your imperfections. To be whole is to appreciate what makes you beautiful both on the surface and beneath it. To be whole is to see scars as a sign of a higher standard or a more in-tact boundary and not brokenness.

Wholeness is boldness, and that's why I'm drawn to this concept of *wabi-sabi*. As you'll see in the coming chapters as we break down our pasts and the uncomfortable and disappointing experiences that have attempted to dull our shine, *wabi-sabi* provides us with a new lens through which to look at life: we are ever-changing and never broken. Your boldness comes from embracing what makes you whole. And to be whole is to embrace imperfection, impermanence, and the fact that your journey is undoubtedly a winding one.

To be bold is to no longer overcompensate in our lives in order to hide imperfection. To be bold is not to hide anything or have multiple versions of yourself from which you pick and choose based on the setting. There's just you... the perfect mix of *wabi* - imperfection - and *sabi* - the beauty of timing and impermanence in your life. Boldness is about freedom from the need to conform, force perception, or define oneself by one thing.

"Wabi-sabi acknowledges that just as it is important to know when to make choices, it is also important to know when not to make choices: to let things be. Even at the most austere level of material existence, we still live in a world of things. Wabi-sabi is exactly about the delicate balance between the pleasure we get from things and the pleasure we get from freedom of things" (Leonard Koren in "Wabi-Sabi: For Artists, Designers, Poets & Philosophers"). [5]

According to Koren, *wabi-sabi* evangelizes the idea that "greatness" exists in the inconspicuous and overlooked details and beauty can be coaxed out of ugliness. It's a state of mind that practices acceptance of the inevitable and the appreciation of the cosmic order. [6]

As we move into unlearning, reinventing, and never going back, consider the things in your life you've been hiding. What are the "ugly" parts of yourself that you rarely address or let see the light of day? What is the "finish" line you've been blindly chasing? What are the expectations and definitions you've been abiding by?

Perhaps it's time to embrace your imperfection in order to be bold? Perhaps what you perceive to be wrong, falling behind, or broken actually contains the source of your boldness? Perhaps detaching from what you've been told is true is the key to finding what is actually true to you? Perhaps embracing change as the only constant in your life is what will deliver the happiness and fulfillment you seek?

There is beauty in your scars. There is beauty in imperfection. There is beauty in embracing your life's timing. *Wabi-sabi*

CHAPTER TWO

The Beautiful Mess Effect

****

Some people will misunderstand you.
Sometimes your heart will be too much for others.

Maybe it's time to commit to your story
instead of trying to fit in someone else's?

Maybe it's time to realize you've been given
magic because you're strong enough to claim it?

Part 1. There's Beauty in Vulnerability

To embrace being true to ourselves, we have to go back to square one of how we perceive what that phrase actually means. We have to go back to the foundation of where our aversion to being "too much" comes from. It certainly comes from a massive amount of conditioning in childhood and adolescence, but practically, it also comes from us having our wires crossed in the way we judge others vs. the way we judge ourselves.

Simply put, we are hypocrites. There, I said it. We are all massive hypocrites. You, me, us - we're all hypocrites in the sense that we perceive other people's vulnerability, openness, honesty, and "too muchness" in way more positive terms than we do our own.

Let's start with the idea of vulnerability. Vulnerability is "an authentic and intentional willingness to be open to uncertainty, risk, and emotional exposure in social situations in spite of fears." [1] Vulnerability is willingness to be "too much," and the reality of actually doing that is we judge ourselves harshly and without question.

"What will others think?"

"I don't want to seem too weird, sensitive, needy, desperate, difficult, etc."

When we look in the mirror and shine a light on our face, the self-judgment is palpable. But in sharp contrast to that self-judgment, we tend to see vulnerability in others as a laudable trait. We appreciate it when other people are honest and open. We tend to love to be around people who light up a room with passion and confidence. We applaud people who are willing to be first and do different things.

Maybe you have a friend you admire because they're the "doesn't give a single f**k" friend, and you watch them in awe when they're willing to do and say things you'd cringe to think of doing yourself? Maybe you look up to your boss who can control a room with a unique combination of poise, humor, and relatability? Maybe you eagerly support someone who creates art, music, or entertainment with an over-the-top brand of weirdness and a carefree attitude?

Why do we judge other people's vulnerability so positively but condemn the same behavior in ourselves? Why do we hold ourselves to an entirely different standard?

Why do we love seeing raw truth and openness in other people, but we're afraid to let them see it in us?

Why are we of a mindset that says, "I want to experience your vulnerability, but I don't want to be vulnerable? I'm drawn to your vulnerability, but repelled by mine?" Why do we revert to thinking and judging from a mindset that says, "Vulnerability is courage in you and inadequacy in me."

Those quoted phrases are from a study titled, "Beautiful Mess Effect: Self-Other Differences in Evaluation of Showing Vulnerability" which was published in the *Journal of Personality and Social Psychology* in 2018. [2]

The "Beautiful Mess Effect"…

The headline from the study is that contrary to how we've been conditioned to think negatively about ourselves, there's something undeniably attractive about our own vulnerability. It's attractive in the sense that other people appreciate it, relate to it, and openly desire it in partners and friends.

People are attracted to real, vulnerable humans.

That's not just a warm and fuzzy thought. The researchers, Anna Bruk, Sabine Scholl, and Herbert Bless from the University of Mannheim in Germany, set out to prove that situations where one might show their vulnerability like confessing romantic feelings, asking for help, or taking responsibility for a mistake are positively judged by others but negatively by ourselves when we're the ones performing them.

The researchers proved this theory through a series of controlled experiments. In the most cringe-inducing experiment, the researchers asked participants to improvise singing a song in front of a jury and asked the jury to rate the performer's vulnerability, courage, poise, etc.

But the researchers didn't actually have the first group sing or be rated by the jury. Right before the performers were told to begin singing, they were asked to rate themselves and their vulnerability in that moment. The results showed they were VERY harsh on themselves - saying they wished they could avoid it, that others would be repelled by it, that it would not be well-received, and that it would be seen as a weakness.

At the same time, they asked the jury to do the same and they basically said the opposite: the singing of the unrehearsed song would be courageous, admirable, and "an act of showing vulnerability - no matter how good it actually was."

In other experiments, the researchers ran hundreds of participants through scenarios where they were asked to display intentional vulnerability or rate someone else's intentional vulnerability. Each time, the participants rated their own vulnerability significantly more negatively than when judging the same behavior in other people.

The vulnerability included tasks such as confessing love for a close friend, revealing the imperfections of their body to others, apologizing first after a fight, asking for help, and admitting having made a mistake. Each time, the self-review was more harsh than when judging the same activities and emotional presentation in others.

"Across a set of six studies, the obtained findings demonstrate consistently that showing vulnerability is perceived more positively when vulnerability is displayed by others rather than by oneself." [3]

It begged the question of: why do we apparently value vulnerability in other people, but we're overly critical of it in ourselves? Why do we consider other people's imperfections and vulnerability a "beautiful mess," but consider it just a mess in ourselves? What they found was pretty interesting and lends some scientific and psychological thinking to a feel-good statement like "vulnerability is attractive."

They found evidence around what they called "construal level." Based on the experiments, they found that when we think about our own vulnerability, we do so very concretely. We construe (interpret or analyze) specifically and with facts. When that's the case, it's deemed to be a low construal level.

For our own vulnerability, we interpret and judge it from a very close, tangible, and concrete perspective - low construal level. But when we think about others, we do the opposite. We think broadly and in an abstract sense - high construal level. [4]

The experiments showed that the more abstract our thinking of vulnerability is, the more positive and admirable we tend to think it is. The more specific and concrete we think of vulnerability, the more negative and judgmental we think it is.

When thinking of our own vulnerability, we are drawn to specific downsides and negative aspects, but when considering the same vulnerability in others, we draw more warm and broad optimistic conclusions about it.

What leads us to be so critical of ourselves and not of others is how close we are to ourselves. Literally. When our minds can find specific memories associated with our own messiness, embarrassment, or failure, we judge ourselves negatively.

That makes sense, right? We are easily able to spot wrongdoings and imperfections from our own "lowlight reels," (aka the opposite of a warm and fuzzy highlight reel of positive memories) and we then can easily extrapolate that thinking to the future and what might happen to us. And, voila, we judge ourselves negatively all because we're so close to ourselves and we arm our negative thinking with specific negative memories.

But when we think of others, we don't have that memory bank, so we think in a more abstract way. As a result, we're more focused on the upside of vulnerability - we leave room for the good instead of assuming the worst.

So, what do we do with this revelation? The conclusion is what I think we want to wholeheartedly agree with, but we struggle to do so in reality. Our flaws, our vulnerability, our true feelings, and our true character - whether we believe it or not - are more attractive than we think. At a minimum, they are not as messy as we think. They are not as detracting as we think.

We've proven that we admire vulnerability in others. We think THEIR "too muchness" and honesty is great. It's attractive. It's humanizing. It's relatable. But when it comes to our own, we adopt the opposite point of view. It's not attractive, it's too much, it's too little, it's crazy. And we use our stored memory banks to support that notion. But the truth of the matter is - within reason, of course - a well-intentioned, compassionate, honest, beautiful mess is attractive. Showing that beautiful mess and acting vulnerably doesn't make you weak, unqualified, or inadequate. To others, it is attractive. To you, it is attractive.

If that's true or if there's a possibility that's true, maybe that can change how we approach presenting ourselves? Maybe we can redefine how we judge ourselves and the willingness we have or lack thereof that comes from our own self-judgment? Maybe we can be kinder to ourselves and embrace being a bit "too much?" How would that make you feel?

How would it feel to be one person on the inside and the same person on the outside?

We need to check our very human assumption that others judge us in the same way we judge ourselves. Just as the researchers proved, it's not true. We've proven with our own affirmation as well: we applaud vulnerability in others. Even though we might judge ourselves harshly, the rest of the world does not.

We are so close to ourselves, our pasts, all of our missteps, all of our mistakes, and all of our thoughts. We are so close to years and years and years of collected data that it's easy to assign negative judgments in the present and the future to things we might do or say. But we rarely do the same to others. We applaud their honesty, we find comfort in it, and we appreciate someone who is real, raw, and authentic.

What would happen if we approached ourselves from that same mentality? What would happen if we approved of the beautiful mess in our lives?

I'm not saying this in a reckless sense. I'm not talking about being out of control, overboard, or irrational. I'm talking about being poised in your realness. Poised in your vulnerability. Poised in speaking what's on your mind. I'm talking about being confident in being "too much." Being a beautiful mess does not make you inadequate, less, or any of the labels we love to assign to ourselves.

What if we assigned the same adjectives we so freely give to others? Brave, courageous, real, authentic, honest, bold…

Consider your own behavior vs. when observing other people's vulnerability. Ask yourself: "Why are they not the same?"

Maybe the key to breaking your own pattern of self-judgment is affirming that how you see yourself is NOT how other people see you?

Maybe that's enough for you to hit pause and reset how you judge yourself? Maybe that's enough to recognize that where you see a mess in yourself, others see a human being. Others see relatability. They see what you see in them: realness and authenticity. And that's attractive.

At the end of the day, that's what we want in friends, partners, and colleagues, right? We don't want fake. We don't want filtered. We don't want watered down. We want real.

You deserve to admire your realness in the same way you do others.

There is beauty in your vulnerability.

Part 2. The Upside of Downsides

I really do think your vulnerability is a superpower. But, maybe you're not convinced? Maybe you haven't warmed up to this idea just yet because you have a memory bank filled with examples of times where you let that superpower shine through and it was thrown back in your face - it was met with rejection, judgment, misunderstanding, etc.

How do we adopt a more eager mentality toward embracing being "too much" in the face of our memories where it wasn't well-received?

Here is a lesson presented by The Flash - a comic book superhero whose power is speed. He's VERY fast. He can do all kinds of crazy things like control molecules and pass through objects because of his speed. But when he's not superheroing, he's a nerdy guy named Barry Allen. Ironically, there's a joke that's written into his non-superhero character that he's always late. He's always that guy who can't seem to ever show up on time.

Contrary to his superhero self that can get anywhere he wants in a flash, he underestimates the time needed to get somewhere in the real world, and so he's the fastest guy on the planet, BUT he has a tendency to be chronically tardy.

I bring this up because it represents the idea that you can have an amazing superpower, BUT it likely comes with a downside. A "flaw." Fast BUT late. Think about that sentence structure for a second. Superpower BUT downside. Talent BUT flaw. Vulnerability as a superpower comes with potential downsides.

You're willing to be vulnerable, BUT maybe that leads you to be rejected often because you're willing to be open and honest first?

The pattern plays out with other superpowers too…

You're highly empathetic, BUT maybe that leads you to give and give and sometimes you don't save enough compassion for yourself? You're incredibly kind and selfless, BUT maybe you've let that kindness be taken advantage of by other people? You're disciplined and motivated, BUT maybe you find yourself neglecting other areas of life - relationships, self-love, mental health, etc.

While those superpowers might be nothing overt like The Flash, being a great athlete, or a MENSA member, they are indeed superpowers... and they come with balance. They come with a potential "flaw." They come with "BUT."

The reality of life is that everything is about balance. You do one thing or you dedicate yourself to one thing and it will inevitably have an impact in other areas of life. But we don't realize this is totally normal, natural, and to be expected, and so when we see "BUT," we freak out and we question our superpower.

We become tempted to give up on it in favor of something that's more comfortable and without the potential "BUT." Or worse, we allow other people to convince us that our superpower is silly, "too much," or "crazy."

I'll list out some superpowers here so we're on the same page:

Kindness, empathy - yep, that's a superpower. Having unwavering high standards - definitely. Being disciplined, motivated, or stubborn about something- absolutely. Being incredibly optimistic- big time. Being weird - yes, my fellow weirdo. Being someone who always asks "why"- yes. Being someone who isn't afraid of embarrassing him or herself - yep.

Superpowers come with potential downsides. That's unfortunately how life works. It's built into the fabric of anything vulnerable, and realizing this is the key to no longer talking yourself out of being "too much."

If you have unwavering high standards and that's you being "too much" - well, sometimes you might think you're alone in the world, you get in your head, or you feel like you're falling behind. Downside. If you're incredibly disciplined, motivated, and stubborn about something you're passionate about - well, sometimes you get obsessed and forget about life outside those things. Consequently, life can pass you by or you let your happiness be dictated by uncontrollable outcomes. Downside.

If you're an incredibly optimistic person - well, sometimes that turns into a defense mechanism where you don't take time to really consider life and what's going on. Sometimes you take risks that aren't justified, you stay in a relationship hoping it will improve only to realize it won't, etc. Downside. If you're someone who always asks "WHY"- well, sometimes that can aggravate others, make them think you think too much, or you overthink things in life. Downside.

I'd say that by most measures - those traits are superpowers. But clearly, they come with potential downsides. And we're acutely aware of the downsides. Maybe they frustrate you?: "Why am I like this? Why do I always see the good in others? Why can't I let this go? What's wrong with me?"

Left unchecked, we consider those completely normal downsides to be flaws. And we run from flaws. We are incredibly averse to downsides in ourselves, and so we revert to comfort and away from being "too much."

I offer this point about balance to encourage you to NOT question your superpower simply because you have memories to reference where it's been taken advantage of, judged, or led you into situations that frustrated you.

We are all given superpowers in life and we should celebrate them - no longer using BUT to justify not letting them shine.

We celebrate the same superpowers in others, and it's time we do the same for ourselves DESPITE the memories we have of the specific instances where that balance was less than enjoyable.

Life is about balance. And yes, sometimes your superpower is going to invite judgment, criticism, heartbreak, etc. and you're going to be tempted to think, "I need to close off, I shouldn't do this, or I need to avoid being hurt."

The world indeed shapes us in heavy ways, but please recognize that no superpower comes without temptation. Realize this and question your inclination to retreat to comfort.

We're all going to be tempted to turn our backs on our superpowers. We're all going to be tempted to close off and become cold because someone treated you that same way. We're all going to be tempted to lower our standards because we're tired of searching and waiting. We're all going to be tempted to chill with our drive and aspirations because we keep getting curveballs and it's easier to lower the bar.

We're all going to be tempted to stop asking "WHY" and just accept life.

Temptations are going to weigh heavily on you and they're going to be specific to the superpower you've been given. Perhaps that's how you ended up living in the gray of life? You let that "BUT" convince you that your superpower is not worth sharing with the world?

**Maybe when you thought you were falling behind…
you just were building something better?**

**Maybe when you thought you were rejected…
you were just being redirected?**

**Maybe when you thought you didn't deserve
them… they didn't deserve you?**

Your superpower - aka being "too much" - has the ability to change your life and change other peoples' lives.

I'm not afraid to say something overly sensitive like, "Kindness can change the world." Or, "Creativity can change the world." Or, "Curiosity" can change the world. It absolutely can. It can change your life. It can deliver what you deserve. It can change your partner's life and it could change the world.

But if you throw it aside because you have a handful of times where it didn't deliver the result you wanted, that's something you'll look back on and regret.

You are wired to be kind, empathetic, driven, curious, bold, and with high standards, etc. Don't let the world rewire you. Don't let your ex rewire you. Don't let your boss, your job, the internet, your friends, or your family rewire you. Don't let your memories rewire you. Reframe.

"Vulnerability is courage in you AND courage in me."

CHAPTER THREE

Whoever Cares More, Wins

****

You know what's attractive?

Someone who believes in their "extra."

Humble but confident, soulful but funny...
someone who takes the last slice of pizza,
knows what they bring to the table, and says
"goodbye" to anyone who doesn't see their worth.

Part 1. "I Don't Want to Seem Desperate"

If you spend any time on social media, you're bound to come across people giving dating advice. That's great! I support it! I, myself, create a lot of dating content and have written books about applying mindfulness to dating.

But eventually, you're bound to come across what I specifically think is the worst dating advice possible, and its impact transcends dating and into the very essence of what it means to "try" in life. The advice usually presents itself in some form of "whoever cares less wins."

"It's better to be the person who cares less. You should match their energy. You shouldn't invest energy, compassion, or interest until they do."

I'm sure you've heard variations of this type of advice, and it's further reflected in the practical "how to" things we're told to do or not do - don't respond to a text right away; that's caring too much. Let them lead. Don't follow up after a date first; that's caring too much. Definitely don't make the first move; that's caring too much.

Care less and you have the power. Care less and you win. Care less and you'll be happier because you're just this happy go-lucky, aloof person who doesn't let someone else's actions or inactions get you down. You won't be disappointed by people when they hurt you, ghost you, or dismiss you because you didn't care in the first place. Care less because that protects you. Sound familiar?

I think that's absolutely ridiculous advice. What a lame, passive, defeated, and low energy way to live your life!

I cringe every time I hear someone say, "I don't want to seem overeager" or, "I don't want to be the one to make the first move," or, "I'm worried I'll come across as too much."

Whoever cares less has all the power... Oof. How did we get to this point? We think to care less is to protect ourselves, and we are wired to protect ourselves. It's a preservation mentality. No shock there. If you don't care, then an outcome can't hurt you. There's no attachment and therefore, no hurt. That person can't hurt you. Disappointment can't hurt you. Rejection can't hurt you. I get that. But think about what living with a preservation mentality really looks like. Is it preservation like we say, or is it a fear-based response?

If you're like most people, at some point in life, you've been disappointed, heartbroken, lost, or hurt, and so you have specific proof that supports the notion you should care less to protect yourself. You have proof that says someone needs to show you they care or are interested BEFORE you show that you care. That way, you don't ever have to put yourself in a position again to be hurt, rejected, or frustrated.

I can buy that at face value. I really can. But at its core, this is really a reflection of fear of repeated experiences. It's fear of experiencing the same hurt again. We care less to protect ourselves because we've learned in the past that caring can be painful. We care less because we don't want to experience those things again. We care less as a means to take back our power. But isn't that the opposite of taking your power back?

When you're not willing to care first, you're living a life in reaction to the world and the people around you. When you're not willing to care first, you're basically asking for permission to do and get what you want. When you're not willing to care first, you're always waiting for someone else to tell you or show you what you should do.

Is that really you taking back your power? Or is it you giving it away even more?

We tend to avoid considering that question because we've developed an assumption that caring too much or caring first means you're desperate.

And society doesn't like desperate people, right? Society has taught us that texting first, trying too hard, showing interest first, or being the first to try is desperate. And so, we've rebranded our fear of being hurt again to something a bit more palatable by saying we don't want to seem "desperate." That social logic supports our innate desire to protect ourselves and is more appealing than saying, "I'm afraid of being hurt again."

"I don't want to seem desperate." That's become the socially acceptable reason we lean on. That's the reason we go with. It's simpler. It's less rooted in anything deeper. That's how we rationalize caring less. But all that mentality does is give away our power. It blocks us in life. It blocks potential. It blocks opportunity. It blocks connection. We need to establish a new standard for ourselves that says caring is the ultimate sign you're in control in your life.

How is being in control of your life, how is going after what you want, and how is speaking your mind... desperate?

How is owning how you feel desperate? How is speaking up first desperate? How is setting the tone for what you expect desperate? It's anything but desperate.

Caring first does NOT make you weak, making the first move does NOT make you desperate, and asking for more does NOT make you needy. It's the clearest sign you're in control of your life.

We've been conditioned to think caring less gives us more power. We think caring less protects us. We think it prevents us from appearing desperate. We think caring less is the key to avoiding hurtful life experiences more than once. We need to flip the script. We need to care MORE.

For two reasons...

The first reason is a soulful reason. Do you want to look back on your life and say, "Good news! I protected myself. I avoided hurtful circumstances. Success."

… but then insert a line of fine print that says, "But I ended up settling, I ended up waiting until someone finally recognized me. I waited for permission to go for it. I waited until energy was given to me."

Do you want to look back and say someone chose you instead of you choosing them? Do you want to look back and say you waited for people and circumstances to give you permission to express yourself?

As nice as it is to be chosen or recognized first, if you look back and realize your life path was handed to you passively because you didn't say how you really felt, you waited three days to text back, or you didn't speak up when you wanted to, what does that really say? It says you likely overlooked a path that was MORE right for you.

Personally, I never want to look back and realize I didn't choose MY path. I don't want to regret waiting around, hiding my true self so as not to scare someone else or to not rock the boat. I don't want to regret passing up on opportunities because I didn't want to appear a certain way. I don't want to live a life motivated by fear.

I know I will regret that! In the moment, it might seem like simple self-preservation, but in retrospect, I can guarantee it's going to be a regret to live from a place of fear. It will be a regret to allow yourself to wait for energy to come your way. It will be a regret to allow yourself to wait for interest to be shown to you. It will be a regret to hold yourself back out of fear of coming across as "desperate."

Whoever cares less won't get hurt as much. I can't argue with that. Statistically, that's probably true.

But here's what I know:

Whoever cares less will regret more.

I fundamentally believe it, and that's the second more practical reason to embrace caring MORE. Whoever cares less will regret more.

Life is about balance. Life is about tradeoffs. So, which do you choose? Be the one who protects themselves but has more to regret looking back? Or be the one who has experienced all flavors of life - good and bad - and have much less to regret?

Do you choose comfort in the present? OK, I understand. But I really do think you're choosing regret when you look back. It might not be an exact regret you can pinpoint, but it will be a deeper, soulful regret that says… "I had so much in the tank, but I never let it out because I was afraid." Yikes.

I want to encourage you (and me) to recognize that it's human and it's OK to want to protect ourselves. Please, protect yourself from instances where you have proof that more energy or effort would be counterproductive or hurtful. Please, remove yourself from situations where you tried but it clearly doesn't deserve more effort beyond that. Please, move past times where you did try first but it wasn't reciprocated. Of course. No chasing beyond that initial effort. Reciprocity and respect is the name of the game.

But I advocate for us to care MORE. I advocate for us to care more… first. I advocate for us to be the first to text, the first to follow-up, the first to be energetic, the first to be honest and vulnerable, the first to stop pretending, the first to embrace being "too much."

I advocate for that for all the reasons above, but also for a very practical reason: it weeds out people who are not right for you. I'm not necessarily talking about dating.

I'm talking about any relationship in your life. I'm talking about your tribe - anyone in your life.

Caring first or caring more is a win/win. If your honesty, your eagerness, or your vulnerability makes someone think you're desperate and that's a turn off for them, you just dodged a major bullet.

Think about it... If you hid those things, if you held yourself back, and if you took the approach of caring less... and you then developed a relationship of any kind with someone (who would've been turned off by your realness in the first place) are you with the right person?

No way. You're with someone you won over by not being real and by not being honest. Is that a life you want? Is that a life you choose?

Practically, as much as it will hurt from time to time, someone who is turned off by you caring more... well, that's great news. You have clear proof in front of you that they are not for you. If they think caring is desperate, that person is not for you. How could they possibly be for you? Why would you even consider hiding yourself in order to win someone over?

You'd agree that you deserve someone who loves you for you, right? You deserve someone who appreciates your true personality and your real emotions, right? When you care less, you're not being that person.

Caring more... Caring how you actually care... Caring an accurate amount... THAT is the real you, and if someone is turned off by that... why would you want to win them over by hiding it? You don't deserve that.

To be clear, caring more definitely opens you up to more rejection, more frustration, and more being misunderstood.

Those are undoubtedly the things we're wired to want to avoid in life, but personally, I will take those temporary experiences over looking back and realizing I'm with the wrong person, I hid myself, I settled, or I watered myself down to a version of myself that I'm not proud of.

As much as I want to avoid being hurt in life, I want to avoid regret more. What about you? I hope you choose a mindset that is motivated by a desire to minimize regret instead of self-preservation that is born of fear.

Be real first, not in reaction to other people.

Part 2. The Power of Your Ego

As with all things in life, embracing being different is easier said than done. It's easy for me to preach being "too much" and to just tell you it's as easy as that. Fear of judgment can be paralyzing. Rejection can be debilitating. Embracing your vulnerability is not an on/off switch you control completely. Life is complicated.

So, here's where I recommend turning to the power of your ego. Yes, your ego - that thing Ryan Holiday says is your enemy. I certainly agree that there is a clear and obvious negative side to your ego, and that is very much your enemy. But I have also learned the power of a specific, more optimistic side of your ego.

There is one side to your ego that says, *"I know everything. I am everything. I deserve everything."* That is your enemy. But there is another side that says, "I am willing to try everything. I am open to everything. I can handle everything thrown my way." That is your friend.

This is the compassionate side to your ego, and it's the force behind being willing to care first and to care more. This side of your ego is the antidote to indifference. This ego says that above all things in life, you are free to be the one who cares first, is extra, or "too much" because you can handle anything that comes next.

"I can handle it."

"I can handle being rejected."

"I can handle unreciprocated feelings."

"I can handle being misunderstood."

"I can handle judgment."

Indifference is a fear-based response in life, but when you tap into the "I can handle it" side of your ego, you become someone who is willing to care and be the first to care, to try, to be vulnerable, who doesn't play games, and who doesn't give into phony "rules" or expectations.

This is a reframe of ego because when we consider ego, we normally think about selfishness, narcissism, apathy, and indifference to others. We think of someone who thinks they're hot sh**, who is loud, annoying, and pompous. We've learned that ego is the enemy of compassion. Ego is an over-inflated sense of importance. I agree. THAT is the bad side of ego. Don't allow that side of you to blossom and don't tolerate it in others. But as with everything in life, there is another side. Balance.

The "I can handle it" side to your ego is powerfully compassionate. It's powerfully empathetic. This side of your ego is what leads you to do more, love more, and care more because it reminds you that you can handle any outcome that comes from being "too much."

It reminds you that you have the character and the vision to not be thrown by someone's criticism of you. It reminds you that you have every right to ask for clarity in a relationship or establish your standards or boundaries, and if it comes across as "extra," so be it. You're only "too much" for someone who isn't enough for you. It reminds you that you can start a business, try new music, art, or writing, and if it's judged or criticized, so be it. You can handle it.

This side of your ego gives you a healthy dose of confidence.

You deserve to know that your energy, your soul, and your intention are rare.

It's not confidence that says, "I'm the greatest, and every word that comes out of my mouth is gospel." No, it gives you the confidence that no matter what, you can handle what comes next. It gives you the confidence to do, feel, and communicate your honesty no matter what because you know that whatever happens or doesn't happen next... you can handle it.

Nowhere in that equation are you being selfish, narcissistic, or full of yourself. You simply know that you can react to what you start. You can react to anything that comes from being "too much."

You can do that because you recognize a powerful universal truth. The universe rewards those who care! The universe rewards those who are NOT apathetic. The universe rewards those who are NOT indifferent to their voice, their emotions, their vulnerability, their passions, or their talent or creativity.

When you combine your ego with a willingness to be vulnerable, you're an unstoppable, compassionate, hopeful, caring force. Your ego inspires you to say how you really feel. Your ego inspires you to be the one to go left when everyone else goes right. Be the one who tries. Because you care. To treat your ability to care with indifference is something you'll regret.

So, I say let your ego out of the cage. Let it out of the cage in a powerfully compassionate way that says, "I'm going to be the one who cares. I'm going to be the one to say how I really feel... because I care. I'm going to be the one to ask that person out first... because I care. I'm going to be the one to post that thing on Instagram... because I care. I'm going to be the one who acts on my creative spirit... because I care. I'm going to be the one who does more... because I care."

Be the person who cares! Be the person who cares more than others. Be the one who acts on curiosity, compassion, and treats indifference like socks with crocs - you just don't have time for it.

Ambition is attractive.
Being independent is attractive.
Loving yourself is attractive.
Having different priorities is attractive.
Saying what you want is attractive.

That is the power of your ego. It puts you in the game. It takes you off the indifferent sidelines of life and gets you playing - even if you are nervous or unsure. And frankly, that is all that matters in life. You put yourself in the game... because once there, you can figure out the rest.

It gives you the incentive to take step one. And you need more step ones in your life! You can figure out step two, but you need that initial step. Step ones are led by ego, compassion, and boldness. That's step one of reaching out to someone you want to connect with. That's step one of asking that person out. That's step one of posting that art you created. That's step one of starting your business, considering another job, moving cities, etc.

That's the power of your ego and that's the power of caring, and when that is your motivation and your vision for your life, I seriously don't see how you can lose.

You can handle anything that comes your way. You can try anything, and you can react to whatever happens next. You can be the person who cares when everyone else says indifference is the way.

You can be the person who doesn't play games when everyone else says that's how it should be. You can be the person who does something different when everyone else says, "No that's not the way it's always been."

That's the power of your ego and your willingness to care MORE.

"I can handle it."

CHAPTER FOUR

Drama and Looking in the Mirror

****

You're a 10 but…

*That's it. You're a 10. You're
not too much or too little.*

*You have a beautiful heart,
kind energy, a powerful voice,
passion, and pizazz for a reason.*

You're exactly who you're supposed to be.

Part 1. At Your Worst...

"If you can't handle me at my worst, you don't deserve me at my best!"

Have you ever heard that phrase? What does your "worst" look like? What are you like when sh** hits the fan? What are you like when you're rejected, betrayed, frustrated beyond belief, or hurt in a way you didn't deserve?

Moments of conflict or drama are a great lens into how we've been conditioned to act and respond in life. Those moments give us the ultimate insight into how we define our roles in the world and a true glimpse into how we see ourselves. Are we victims? Are we at the mercy of an unfair world? Are we never at fault? Do we avoid truthful and honest self-reflection about our role in our own frustration?

To escape the gray of life and tap into the most honest and compassionate aspects of who we are, we must look at ourselves in the context of our "worst" and how we got to this point.

It's never too late to let go of baggage that was never yours to carry.

It's never too late to see the good in yourself that you always see in others.

Let's turn to Stephen B. Karpman, M.D whose "Drama Triangle" concept might provide us with insight into how we've been conditioned to see and react to life around us. [1] Karpman is a psychiatrist and the creator of what he calls the "Drama Triangle." It's basically an inverted triangle that outlines three people- the Rescuer, the Persecutor, and the Victim.

Each role describes how one might respond to conflict in life. Conflict = drama or frustration in relationships, friendships, work environments, rejection, betrayal, etc.

Conflict describes anything that makes your blood boil or hurts you in an emotional way.

The Rescuer, the Persecutor, and the Victim...

The roles describe how we innately respond to drama, and more importantly, how it likely came to be that way via some form of conditioning. It's similar to attachment styles - how we've been conditioned to exist in relationships (avoidant, anxious, dismissive, etc.) - but these roles are specific to conflict.

Let's review each and see what we can learn from looking at ourselves specifically through the lens of conflict. It's important to note that you can assume more than one role in life. You might assume one specific role when it comes to family drama, another in romantic relationships, and another at your job.

Let's start with the Rescuer. The Rescuer wants to "help" or "rescue" others. Amidst conflict, the Rescuer is driven to fix others, but in doing so, they often neglect their own needs by focusing all of their energy on others' needs. In a darker evolution of this role, this person often starts with good intentions to help, but that desire can change to an effort to control and manipulate others. It can lead the Rescuer to have a subconscious need to feel validated through that control. [2]

This role is fascinating because this person usually has their own life issues that need attention, but they prioritize helping others as an escape. They exhaust themselves by doing this and they feel guilty when they're not "rescuing." Perhaps you can relate to this? Taking on someone's problems as your own? Not being happy unless someone else is healed and fixed? Needing to be their go-to helper? Ignoring your own needs and truth?

At their core, Rescuers' desire to help others reflects a deep-seeded desire to belong and to be validated. As a result, their worth comes from how much they can give and give and give, and they tend to avoid their own feelings by focusing on others. They use conflict, drama, and a need for resolution to connect with others.

According to the Drama Triangle theory, this behavior is born during childhood and upbringing. A rescuer usually inherits this "I can fix you" mentality as a result of being smothered by parents, not having been given the leeway to lean into their own self-care, or not having been given independence or much freedom to love themselves. [3]

"I can fix you. I can help you. I can save you."

Obviously, that might sound like a noble intention, but at best, it can become a distraction from one's own problems, and at worst, it can become a manipulation tactic. Part two of this book is dedicated to actions we can take to challenge such conditioning, but for now, consider the description I just gave. Do you tend to distract yourself from your own issues by throwing all your worth and value into fixing someone else?

Next up is the Persecutor... The Persecutor is one who tends to blame others amidst conflict. They usually resort to saying someone else is the cause of the issue at hand. "It's YOUR fault. YOU did this! How could YOU do this?!"

The Persecutor protects themselves by putting others down, and this tendency is also born in childhood or adolescence by helicopter or overly strict parents who were always right and ruled with absolute authority.

It can also be a product of abuse in childhood where now in adulthood you're always on the defensive and you perceive that you're always being attacked in some way.

The result of this subconscious defense mode is you're always looking for evidence that you need to defend yourself. [4]

Much like the example set for you during your upbringing, the Persecutor becomes overly critical of others, casts blame, finds fault, and tries to control. Ultimately, this response comes from a lack of worth. The Persecutor defends themselves by using the thing they never had growing up - authority and control - and they rationalize their behavior as a way to strike back against those who they perceive hurt them.

While the Rescuer is a fixer, the Persecutor is a blamer, and much like the Rescuer is using "fixing" to distract themselves, the Persecutor is doing the same with blame. They don't want to address feelings of worthlessness or inadequacy, and so they use authority and blame to overpower others.

Can you relate to this yourself? Do you feel the need to be in control? Do you tend to project a sense of superiority as a defense mechanism? Do you judge others harshly? Do you struggle to be honest with yourself and your true vulnerability? Do you deny deny deny?

Lastly, the Victim...This is THE essential role in any conflict. For there to be the Persecutor or the Rescuer, there has to be the Victim. There has to be someone who feels powerless and unable to change the outcome. The interesting thing about this role is that the victim can also become the Persecutor or the Rescuer.

The Victim has a mentality of "poor me," but transcends that by blaming others for their pain (becoming the Persecutor) or escaping their own victimhood by "helping" others (becoming the Rescuer). [5]

The Victim feels helpless. They feel lost and unable to change anything about their own circumstances. The Victim might be attracted to the Rescuer so they can be saved. Or they might stay the Victim as a result of being blamed by the Persecutor.

Much like the other two roles, the Victim neglects self-awareness and self-love. They distract themselves from their own abilities by assuming they are totally unfixable, broken, or unlovable. This conditioning is also rooted in childhood. Fear of abandonment, lack of love and self-love presents itself in the Victim, which leads to feeling permanently unworthy. They don't stand up for themselves, they believe the past is an indicator of the future, and they feel their needs are not real. [6]

This can further manifest in anger, self-blame, and lack of fulfillment, but ultimately much like the other roles, the Victim doesn't take much responsibility for their feelings or actions therein.

Which of these can you relate to? All of them in some form? One more than the others? Why do I bring up this triangle? In order to step into your most bold and authentic self, we must challenge how we've gotten to a point where our most bold and authentic self is hidden beneath a routine of conditioned behavior. Our response to drama in life is the most conditioned behavior, and it needs to be examined.

The goal here is to challenge ourselves as thoroughly as possible. I highly recommend therapy to unpack these concepts thoroughly, but for now, the goal is to acknowledge that we have become robots to our conditioning. As a result, we rarely give thought to breaking free of how we usually act, speak, or respond.

We need to ask ourselves powerful questions to break free of our learned responses in life. What in your upbringing conditioned these responses?

Certainly, we can't put all the responsibility of our current state on our upbringing, but I'd ask you to carry a thought in the back of your mind as we continue to peel back the layers: what is the weight you carry with you in your adult life that you learned in your childhood?

Maybe you had a parent who withheld affection from you when you misbehaved or made a mistake? They didn't offer support or comfort when you needed it? Maybe you had parents who placed burdens and responsibilities on your shoulders that were far too heavy or serious for your age? Maybe you had parents who never gave you the quality time and affection you needed? They blurred the line between friend and parent offering little by way of example or structure? Maybe you had very controlling parents who didn't let you show your feelings or express heavy emotions? Maybe you had overly strict parents who made you feel guilty for feeling a certain way, acting out of interest, curiosity, or happiness? Maybe you had parents who did those things because they thought they were protecting you?

What assumed truths and conditioning do you carry with you that cause you to assume the role of the Rescuer, the Persecutor, or the Victim?

Is it that you need to suppress how you feel and focus on how someone else feels instead? Is it that their feelings are more valid than your own? Is it that you need to control every outcome, and it's OK to assume different identities and worldviews to do so? Is it that you're not worthy of someone's love and affection as you really are? Is it that any affection given to you is a controlling tactic and shouldn't be trusted? Is it that you're better off hiding aspects of yourself in favor of fitting in?

These are big questions, but the answers to these types of questions hold the answers to WHY you assume the role you do. I can offer you some initial guidance, but from here, it's up to you to take a good hard look in the mirror.

If you resort to being the Rescuer, address your problems first. Take time to heal. Try journaling. Go to therapy. Talk about your childhood. Learn what triggers you.

Challenge yourself to stop rationalizing giving and giving and giving until you've actually taken time to give to yourself.

If you resort to being the Persecutor, you have to challenge yourself to stop blaming others. Stop looking outside before looking within. This role in particular is all about self-awareness. WHY are you avoiding being vulnerable with yourself? Why do you feel the need to be right? Why do you feel threatened?

And lastly, the Victim. If this is you, learn to go within. Show yourself that you are powerful. Challenge the assumptions you've made about yourself that you're unworthy, unchangeable, or unlovable. "Poor me?" Is it really "poor you" or do you just assume it is? Address the conditioning or trauma that makes you feel powerless. Don't self-blame and find a way to be proud of yourself. In some way, I think we can all relate to being the Victim, and we'll focus more on aspects of that condition in coming chapters.

At the end of the day, removing yourself from any role in the Drama Triangle is about awareness first and understanding second. It's about realizing that these habits and inclinations are a result of years of conditioning followed by years of routine and continued behavior.

It's time we allow ourselves to let go of weight that is no longer ours to carry, people who are no longer for us, and assumptions that dull our optimism.

Forgive yourself for having these inclinations, forgive yourself for accepting them as normal, and draw a new boundary. That's a new boundary that challenges your knee-jerk reactions in life.

How can you move away from your robot reaction mode and toward your most vibrant, bold, and free self?

Part 2. The Best Revenge in Life

I just threw a doozy of a question at you. I basically asked you, "Why are you like this?"

I asked you to challenge your conditioning. I asked you to consider how pain and hurt has shaped you. I asked you to consider yourself when you're at your most vulnerable and emotional - disappointed, rejected, attacked, etc.

Finding answers or clarity to those questions is no small task, and I hope you don't feel too much pressure to do so. You can be driven by a desire to challenge yourself and your conditioning, but also balance it with pride.

It's so easy to place enormous weight on your shoulders and to beat yourself up for not measuring up to your own potential. It's easy to feel lost, down on yourself, disappointed in yourself, and chronically critical of everything you do or don't do. We put sooooo much pressure on ourselves to be more, and we're always striving for that "moreness."

Don't get me wrong, I think that's great. Being self-motivated, driven, and averse to settling is a great quality. Frankly, it's the foundation for this very book and the basis for escaping the gray in life.

But if we're not giving ourselves more credit WHILE we're out here living and loving, it becomes a self-defeating cycle where you feel lost, that you're not rising to the occasion, or that you're letting your younger self down... and that weight follows you around like a shadow of disappointment.

We need balance in our inner life. We need a balance of eagerness to change... gratitude for who we are, and the potential we have to let that shine further. We need a balance between wanting to challenge who we are and the gray we've allowed ourselves to live in AND giving ourselves credit for the glowing aspects of ourselves.

We need to highlight and let shine the great aspects of who we are equally as often as we need to focus on the parts of us that need work and reinvention.

You should be proud of who you are no matter how much work you still have to do.

**You should be proud of yourself
for how far you've come.**

I think THAT is the key to living a fulfilling life - finding a way to be proud of yourself amidst all the things you're still going after, the ways you're still growing, and the ways you're still healing.

We have to find a way to be proud of ourselves - even if we're single and we don't want to be, even if we're not working our dream job at the moment, even if our art, music, or startup hasn't blown up yet, even if we disappoint ourselves frequently and haven't found a way to stop retreating to our familiar role in the Drama Triangle.

Amidst the inner work we're doing, we have to find a way to be proud of who we are NOW. One way I've found to do this is to consider the phrase, "The best revenge in life is to not be like your enemy." You've heard that saying before, right? How can we use this phrase to give us the balance we need in life?

Ask yourself this: "What would the enemy of YOU look like?" I hope you don't have any literal enemies in life, so let's assume your enemy is the opposite of you. It's the opposite of who you are, what you stand for, and for what you want in life.

My enemy - the opposite of Case Kenny - would be someone who is critical of others and themselves, who is not motivated, is lazy, mean, has no empathy, is superficial, and who doesn't do what they say they're going to do.

What would your enemy look like? Describe the person you don't want to be. Describe the person you don't want to become. Describe the opposite of YOU.

Describe the person that is the version of you if you gave up on all the things that are important to you. That's the version of you if you took all the lessons you've learned, all the standards you have, your vision for life, your goals, the ethics you live by, and the best aspects of your personality... and you threw them in the trash. Is that person someone who is lazy? Who is critical of others? Who gives up easily? Is it someone who is selfish? What gives you "the ick" in a person? What can someone do that's a huge turnoff? Describe that. Describe the ick.

Literally try this right now. If the best revenge in life is to not be like your enemy, then it logically follows that when you're not like that person, when you don't give into temptation, and when you don't turn cold in the face of life... that's something to be proud of.

**In case no one told you today...
ambition and high standards
look good on you.**

Long story short, you should be proud of yourself for NOT being a certain way. It's great to push yourself to be MORE, do MORE, and check off MORE things on your bucket list, but while you're working on that... be proud of who you are. That pride will lead you to find more incentive to let the great aspects of yourself shine! It will give you more incentive to tap into the aspects of you that you refuse to let go of: your kindness, your quirks, your personality, your drive... aka your "too muchness."

You haven't given up on those things! They might be hidden beneath a facade of negative acceptance and learned behavior, but they're there! You are not your enemy, and that is great news!

Enemy is a strong word, but if it's used to describe someone who has given into the temptations YOU work so hard to resist, if this person has given up on the things YOU are working so hard to do and become and have… it's a good description! They're your enemy. Because you're the opposite of them and they want you to become like them! They want you to be on their level. They want to pull you down! But you haven't given up on the things that are important to you and that matters!

Amidst all the things you haven't done, the things you've tried and failed to do, the times you still disappoint yourself… you're still not those negative things you listed out.

You're not your enemy. You haven't become your enemy. You refuse to be like your enemy. You refuse to give up. You refuse to be cold. You work hard to be self-aware and bold. You work hard to love others, to support others, and to go after your dreams. That's a pretty great thing, right?

You deserve to give yourself more credit WHILE you work to unlearn. You deserve to give yourself more credit WHILE you work to give yourself more second chances. You deserve to give yourself more credit WHILE you reinvent aspects of yourself. This is fuel that will keep you going.

And perhaps in the process of considering this, you'll find a reason to let your most vibrant side show more often. That is what this balance offers. A balance between more and gratitude. A balance between going fast and going slow.

Use this foundation of pride to keep yourself going when it gets tough to challenge your conditioning and rewire how you react to people and conflict in life.

Leaning on this idea of "you are not your enemy" can give you a sense of pride. You are not like your enemy. That path is easy.

It's easy to let life beat you up to the extent that you give up on the things that are important to you. It's easy to do that. It's easy to hide your most vibrant colors in favor of a duller shade of gray. It's safer there.

But you haven't hidden yourself in so many areas of life, and you have so many more parts of yourself to show. And that is something to be proud of.

The best revenge in life is to not be like your enemy...

CHAPTER FIVE

Gratitude

****

In case no one told you,
inner peace looks good on you.

Ambitions and high standards look good on you.

Hot, smart, and worthy looks good on you.

You're the perfect mix of kind heart,
weird sense of humor, and
passion to live life to the fullest.

Part 1. What You Know vs. What You Don't Know

To let our most bold selves see the light of day, we must learn to take back control of our thoughts. We must shift our focus from all the things we DON'T know, the things we DON'T have, and the question marks that linger in our minds to the opposite of those things. We must shift our thoughts and intentions to the things we DO know, the things we DO have, and the exclamation marks we HAVE written in our lives. Doing so allows us to lean into the most true and vibrant aspects of ourselves.

Let's shift from "?" to "!."

I don't know about you, but if I leave my thoughts unsupervised, they tend to lead me in a draining direction - reminding me of all the things I don't have, the things I haven't done, the places I haven't traveled to, the words I haven't heard, etc.

It's important, of course, to spend time in those particular mental spaces - that's how you grow and come to do great things - but we deserve peace and centeredness in our thoughts. We deserve to take back control and not play an active role in making ourselves feel bad for what we don't yet have. Staying in that headspace of shame is what solidifies our learned behavior and ongoing residence in the gray of life.

We can train ourselves to take back our energy by no longer loitering in that space of lack. We can redirect our thoughts from what we don't have, the places we haven't been, and the words we haven't heard to the opposite - the things we have done, the places we have been, and the words we have heard.

This is a powerful shift, and practically, I'm talking about gratitude. But it's not gratitude in the sense of just sitting down and listing out all the things you're grateful for. I'm talking about nurturing a powerful sense of personal pride.

I'm talking about resisting the urge to see a 10/10 model on Instagram in the Maldives and guilt yourself - "I've never been there. I need to be there. Why am I not like her?!" I'm talking about resisting the urge to see that ripped person at the gym and thinking less about yourself because you're not them. I'm talking about resisting the urge to feel FOMO and like you're a loser when you decide to stay in on a Friday night alone. I'm talking about resisting the urge to feel like you're a failure in your career because you haven't made Vice President yet.

I'm talking about pride. I'm talking about taking back your thoughts - away from lack and to what you have and what you know. That's away from what you don't yet have - the dream job, the perfect body, the six-figure check, the car, the confidence. That's away from the experiences you haven't had yet or the relationship that's eluded you. That's away from the question marks that continue to dig at you...

... and to what you do know and what you have experienced.

That's back to the travels you HAVE had. That's back to the progress you HAVE made in the gym. That's back to the things you HAVE learned in your dating life. That's back to the understanding of yourself you HAVE developed over the years.

This is a powerful shift for you in moments where you're tempted to think the things you lack mean you're less. It's powerful for you in moments where you're tempted to think the question marks in your life outweigh what you do have and the exclamation marks you have written.

It's important, of course, to address lack in your life and to address the question marks that need clarity.

That's what mindfulness is all about - leaving nothing left unexamined, asking WHY, and moving in the direction of finding more, better, different, or simpler.

But as with all things, we need balance. In this case, we need to develop a powerful sense of personal pride in order to live our most bold lives. We need to remind ourselves of the exclamation marks we DO have in our lives. Those are exclamation marks that were formerly question marks, but WE turned into exclamation marks.

We have made more progress than we think. We have learned more than we think. We have grown more than we think, and if we're honest, we've seen and experienced more than we think. We need to remind ourselves of those facts.

The world is a better place with you in it.

In the moments where the lack and question marks nag at you and where they threaten your inner peace and self-esteem… let's check that feeling: "OK, I don't have the answer right now. But here's what I do have…"

There is peace in considering how far you've come. Think of how much you've learned about yourself and think of how your confidence HAS grown. Think about that. Seriously think about that. Give yourself some credit! Otherwise, what's the point?

If we never take time to consider the exclamation marks we've created in our lives and we only focus on the constant stream of question marks we want to tackle… What's the point? There will always be something. There will always be a new thing that eludes you. There will always be more question marks around the corner.

Personally, I am driven by that because that's what makes life worth living - growth, goals, accountability, high standards, and expectations. But if we don't take time to let what we have done, seen, felt, and accomplished shine through… what is the point? That's why we're on the earth. To celebrate those things. Point them out and let them shine more brightly!

That's pride. Unforced. Just you being real with yourself about what you HAVE done, seen, felt, and accomplished. That's real-world pride amongst real-world growth and real-world goals. That's pride where you're out at a bar and you're feeling a bit socially anxious, and your friend is going up to everyone and is the life of the party and you're thinking to yourself, "Why can't that be me? I'll never be that confident."

Your pride says it's great to push yourself out of your comfort zone, but you've come this far. Think of the confidence you DO have and what you DO bring to the table. That's pride where you remind yourself how far you have come from getting that entry level job to being sales director even if you're feeling you really need to be VP before you'll be happy and financially secure. That's pride where you remind yourself how much it means to you to be able to run a sub 7-minute mile or bench 225 even if you're not totally in love with your body just yet. Balance.

The balance between what you don't have and what you do have. The balance between what you have seen and experienced and what you haven't yet. The balance between how you have loved and have been loved and how you still want to love and be loved.

What DO you know?

Part 2. "I Don't Know"

Now seems like a good time to address our innate human desire to always have ALL the answers in life. That pressure is what gets in the way of us being proud of ourselves and practicing gratitude. We put so much pressure on ourselves to know everything - to have all the dots connected, to have a master plan, and to have all the answers in life.

Being curious and driven is great, but there's a difference between searching for clarity in our lives and obsessing over needing the answers.

Obsessing over knowing why someone broke up with you, why someone ghosted you, why someone rejected you, why someone didn't give you the time of day… Obsessing over knowing the correct path to accomplishing something… Obsessing over finding the blueprint, the exact way, or the exact yes… Obsessing over connecting the dots moving forward…

The pressure to have the answers to those questions is heavy!

Early in life, it's easy to get the basics down. You get the correct answers to a lot of life's early questions quite easily. You go to school, you learn about what it takes to get good grades, please that person, graduate, you know what $a2 + b2 = c2$ is all about, and you get photosynthesis on lockdown. You figure out how to get a job, rent an apartment, and maybe buy a car. OK, cool.

But then you get into the real meat and potatoes of life and suddenly, the "correct" answers aren't so easy to come by. Why do you feel lost in your career? Why did that relationship have to end? Why did you fail at the new thing? What does it take to be happy? To be successful? Why do you resort to being "the Victim" so often? Life's big questions. Adult questions. Questions that reflect the confusing reality of life.

There's something uniquely human about the way we go about facing those questions. We look around and we knee-jerk assume that anyone who appears objectively happy, fulfilled, or successful has found the exact answers to those questions. THEY know the blueprint. THEY are happy and successful. THEY have the a2 + b2=c2 equivalent of real life.

And there YOU are - with a long list of questions and question marks floating around your head. And so, you feel behind. You feel confused. You feel lost. In those instances, it's so easy to retreat to comfort, to learned behavior, and further into the gray. But we have to resist that temptation! We have to take the pressure off for a moment.

Yes, always be asking yourself WHY. That is mindfulness, and I love that kind of introspection. That's self-therapy. But beyond that, it's OK to not have all the answers right now. You're making progress and that's all that matters. I refer to this as being "lost in the right direction." Say it with me:

"I am lost in the right direction."

It's OK to say, "I don't know" and just leave it there. In fact, I find that allowing yourself to not have all the answers is how you end up finding them.

I want to encourage us all to stop putting so much pressure on ourselves to find the answers and to know the exact path of our futures right now. The saying I like to reference is that, "Life has to be lived moving forward but can only be understood looking back."

As much as you'd like it to be otherwise, the timing of understanding your life is not your choice. It comes with time. It comes with experience. It comes when you embrace being confused. It comes with healing. It comes when you let go of looking for answers. It comes when you embrace being willing to turn a page even if you didn't understand the last one.

It comes when you're willing to write a new chapter, create your own closure, or take a step forward even when you're still a bit hung up on the last one. It comes when you give yourself a second chance. It comes when you're willing to unlearn what you thought was true.

Life is a series of chapters, and your happiness is tied to how many pages you're willing to turn. It's tied to the grace you carry with you as you move from chapter to chapter and the humility you display when you recognize it's time to move on.

What holds us back in life? What holds us in place? What causes us to overthink things to the point of paralysis? It's our lack of willingness to simply turn the page and say, "I don't know" and be OK with that right now.

But we are so averse to saying that! We don't want to be that "lost" person because in our minds, everyone else has the answers and we need to NOT be that loser who doesn't know. And so, we put enormous pressure on ourselves to know. But there's something beautiful about simply saying, "I don't know."

When you embrace that, you give yourself freedom to just be. You give yourself freedom to be lost… in the right direction. There's something beautiful about not knowing. There's something beautiful about not having all the answers. There's something beautiful about embracing the journey knowing that you're ever-evolving.

Maybe you've heard the saying, "Losing yourself is the best way to find yourself."

I used to laugh at that. What a silly thing to say! But, from my experience, it's the most liberating thing I've ever learned to embrace. When you put pressure on yourself to have all the answers right now, you start to attach yourself to certain timelines, standards, and motivations that ARE NOT yours. You let the conflict of should vs. intuition rush you.

I'm sure you've felt that conflict before. That's the conflict between your honest intuition and the SHOULDS in your life. That's the conflict between your "too muchness" and the SHOULDS in your life.

You SHOULD know what you're doing. You SHOULD know what your career path looks like. You SHOULD know what your soulmate looks like in life. You SHOULD know what you're looking for. A partner who does xyz SHOULD make you happy. A job that pays you xyz SHOULD make you fulfilled. Dressing, acting, and speaking a certain way SHOULD make you happy.

A conflict exists between those SHOULDS and what our "too muchness" is begging us to explore (more on that in chapter seven). That's being "too much" in any sense that is different from those SHOULDs. But oftentimes, the pressure we've put on ourselves drowns out that inner voice and voila, here we are attaching ourselves to ideas, standards, and timing that are simply not true for us.

Find peace in being willing to say: "Right now, I don't know."

... and be OK with it. It means being OK with unfinished chapters. It means being OK with unanswered questions. It means being OK with living without a roadmap. Right now. Not forever. In this moment. In this season of your life.

Doing this is how you give your soul the experiences and the pressure-free environment to actually find the finished chapters, the answered questions, and the timing that makes sense for YOU.

Practically, I'm just encouraging you to be open-minded and to lessen the pressure you're accustomed to living with. If you don't know, don't know and leave it right there.

Don't let pressure attach you to the first thing that makes the slightest sense. Don't create a standard, a goal, or a blueprint from the first thing you're told is right.

Stay open-minded. You don't need all the answers right now because the freedom to not need the answers is how you find answers that are truly yours. ... not the answers that you borrow from someone else. ... not the answers you feel pressured to say you've found because you're getting older and feel left behind. YOUR answers. Uniquely yours. Based on YOUR life, YOUR experiences, and YOUR intuition.

It's a beautiful thing in life to be able to look back and say, "I didn't pressure myself. I was willing to not know so that eventually I will know for certain."

That means you don't go crawling back to the person who at one point made sense. That means you don't accept the first YES or the first opportunity because you see other people saying that's the right way. That means you don't go back to what's comfortable... That means you lean into life. You don't sit back. You don't give up.

Embrace "I don't know."

Part 3. Is It "Lack" or Is It "Transition?"

While we're embracing this season of reinvention, giving ourselves more credit for what we do have while striving for more and embracing "I don't know," we have to learn an important distinction. We have to learn the difference between the word "lack" and the word "transition."

Lack - the state of being without.

Transition - the process of changing from one condition to another.

We confuse these two words so often that it's no wonder we allow what we don't have to act as proof that we're unworthy of more. We have to learn to relabel what we "lack" or the things we've "lost" in life. Those are reflections of transition. End of story. The end of one chapter means another chapter is starting. The lack of one thing in life means we're on our way to a different version of it. We're simply in a state of transition.

Let's talk about what transition means. I'm not talking about life transitions (aka changes) that YOU decide to embark on- changing a job, changing cities, deciding a relationship isn't working for you, etc. I'm talking about the transitions given to you or the ones you're forced to embrace - you're broken up with, something changes with your job, your family, your friends, etc.

Those are transitions you didn't choose. That's a change from being in a relationship to being single, that's a change from working a job to no longer working there, that's a change from loving yourself to doubting yourself, that's a change in your friendships, etc.

Most of the time, we see those moments as a reflection of loss and lack. We think our life has a big gaping hole in it and the longer it remains vacant, the more we affirm the negative assumptions we have about ourselves.

"I'm unlovable. I'm a failure. I'm too weird. I'm too old."

The most powerful thing we can do WHILE we work for more, better, or different in life is control the assumptions we make. It's powerful to NOT allow our human, reactive mind to assume that change is bad, that different means worse, or that lack or loss is permanent.

Ask yourself this:

Is this LACK or is this TRANSITION?

Is this LOSS or is this TRANSITION?

The reason I find this question so powerful is because it allows you to pause and question where the discomfort of change is coming from. Unexamined discomfort is what causes us to arrive at negative conclusions about change in life, so it's important we challenge it.

Change is always going to be uncomfortable because by definition, change is going from something that was routine and normal to something new. And, of course, that is uncomfortable. As humans, we tend to associate discomfort with the negative. That's how we're wired. But intuitively, we know that not all change is negative. We know that discomfort can be a powerful catalyst for amazing happiness and inner peace.

So how can we prove to ourselves that the discomfort we feel from change given to us in life can be a positive one?

Specifically, how can we prove to ourselves that discomfort is a sign of transition and not permanent lack or loss?

I'm sure you can think of examples in your life where your growth was literally only the result of change - changing from high school to college, changing from working that summer job to finally working your big boy or big girl job, changing from not working out to working out and finding some confidence that way, etc. We have so many examples where our growth was the result of change. But in thinking about those examples, you probably chose the ones where YOU decided to change. You chose the examples where YOU broke up with your ex, YOU changed jobs, YOU moved cities, etc.

In these moments of reflection, it's easy to sit down and say, "Yes, change is good." But what about the changes you didn't want in the first place? Why can't we apply the same logic to those? Mindfulness is about logic. It's about applying the same rules in life whether it's a good scenario or a bad scenario. For instance, if we have proof and believe that life can go from 100 to zero quickly... why can't we believe that life can also go from 0 to 100 quickly as well?

If we believe in bad karma that comes about as a result of negative action... why can't we believe in good karma that comes from compassionate, good, and kind actions?

If we tend to internalize Murphy's law in life and think that the worst will happen to us... why can't we flip it and say the best can happen to us? Logic. And it's the same when it comes to change in life and the assumptions we make as a result.

We have proof that change can be good - the change WE started. Why can't we believe the change given to us can be good as well? Why can't we believe the change given to us is a reflection of transition instead of lack or loss? Why can't we believe the change given to us is a sign that we're now in between two things? We're in between something that wasn't right for us and the future which holds something that is right for us?

Can you push yourself to try this? Can you believe the future holds something better for you and that starting over is the key to finding it? Is it loss or is it transition? Is it lack or is it transition?

Lack is only lack and loss is only loss if you decide this is the end of your story. But if you decide it's not, you're simply in a state of transition. You're in-between two chapters in life, and the discomfort you feel is the discomfort of moving past something that wasn't for you. You're in between A and B. You're in between relationships, jobs, people, and places.

Discomfort is a sign. It's a positive sign that something wasn't right for you, but there is something right for you and it lies beyond the state of transition. Transition means movement. It means upgrade. It means evolution.

The only way it's true loss or lack is if you decide this is the last page of the last chapter of your life story. You don't believe that, do you? You don't believe this is your final chapter? If you're tempted to say you do, I'd challenge you to prove it. Seriously prove to me that this is it! Prove to me that you have NOTHING left in the tank, you're NOT willing to try again, you're giving up, you have NOTHING to offer the world, a partner, a job, a friend, etc.

That's heavy, but I know you'd struggle to actually prove that. Take a break, take the pressure off, say, "I don't know," and affirm that this is not it. "This is not my final chapter."

When that's the case, it's impossible that change given to you in life is anything but transition. You are simply in a state of transition. This is not your final chapter. Far from it. To be your boldest and most vibrant self, you have to be willing to start new chapters and embrace change - both the change you initiate, and the change given to you in life.

Is it lack or is it transition?

CHAPTER SIX

Choosing Yourself

****

*How amazing is it to realize you
can be more than one thing in life?*

*You can be an introvert, an extrovert,
a dog walker, CEO, author, yoga instructor,
pastry chef, musician, ninja, astrologer, comedian,
sommelier, artist, poet, photographer, tarot card
reader, tour guide, film critic, and a talk show host.*

*Your story doesn't need to look like everyone else's.
Speak your mind, smile, laugh, dream, be curious,
and chase your own vibrant version of life.*

Part 1. The Reverse Uno Card

"If your identity is centered around being loved and appreciated by others, you will never really come to know yourself." [1]

That's from the writing of Maryam Hasnaa, and I absolutely love it. Whether we realize it or not, we tend to think self-love is a series of steps. You love them, they love you, and then finally, you love yourself.

We look to others to validate that we're lovable and that we're enough to finally give ourselves that gift. That backwardness in thinking leaves us wishing and waiting. It leads us to see ourselves through the eyes of others rather than through our own eyes. Their eyes = eyes that judge, eyes that apply labels, eyes that define our "enoughness" instead of us defining it for ourselves.

We think that if we just love someone harder, if we just work for that company harder, if we just hustle harder, support harder, commit harder, that will then come back to us in the form of self-love. We think that person will do the same to us or that company will do the same for us, and through that process, we will feel the same way about ourselves. We see outward validation as a sign that we're worthy of our own inner admiration. We think self-love is something that is given to us in the form of a permission slip from someone or something else - a person, company, recognition, etc.

Of course, we recognize that statement couldn't be further from the truth. Self-love is the ultimate inside job and not a three-step process that we've been conditioned to chase.

One, two, three... You love them, they love you, you love you? You support them, they support you, you support you? You choose them, they choose you, you choose you? Life just doesn't work like that. You have to start with you.

It's not selfish to reverse the order of what we've assumed is the correct path to self-love. It's not selfish or narcissistic to switch your focus back to you. You love you... You support you... You choose you...

That's finally switching from wanting to be appreciated and loved by others to appreciating and loving yourself. It's finally giving yourself the same love, respect, and positive intention you give others so freely.

I call this "The Reverse Uno Card Mindset." I don't know if you've played Uno recently, but just as a refresher, the reverse uno card basically reverses the direction of play. So, instead of playing left to right, it reverses to right to left. Reverse.

This mindset does exactly that. It recognizes that before we make time, love, commitment, or compassion for other people in the hopes it's returned to us and we can finally give ourselves the gift of self-love... we need to carve out that same time, love, commitment, and compassion for ourselves.

We have to please ourselves. We have to love ourselves. We have to commit to ourselves. We have to cheer for ourselves. We have to be our own hype person.

You look happier since you started loving yourself in the same way you've always loved others.

I'm not talking about withholding love or kindness from others, but we need to recognize that the more we try to please others without first loving ourselves, the further we get from learning what it means to love ourselves. We need to give to ourselves first what we want from others.

This isn't a narcissistic or selfish practice. This is you returning to what YOU deserve. This is you embracing the pride you built in the last chapter and actually taking it out into the world. This is you deciding you are enough. Reverse.

Part 2. You Are More Than "Enough"

Everything great in your life comes down to how much you believe you're worth.

That makes sense, right? When you know the value of something, it changes what you're willing to do with it. If you own an expensive sports car - let's say a Ferrari - you probably know it's worth ~$200K on the market. You know the value, and so you wouldn't lend it to someone without considerable thought and assurance. You wouldn't sell it unless you had a great offer that recognized its market value. You'd keep it clean and locked up at night. You'd protect it.

It's the same with YOU. When you know YOUR worth, you don't entertain less. If you believe you deserve a partner who chooses you just as you choose them, you don't wait around for someone who is unsure about you. If you believe you're talented and bring a lot to the table, you don't hesitate to speak up, tell that joke, or post that selfie. If you believe you're capable of making an impact in the world, you don't doubt your ability to at least start a business, play your music, or create your art.

I think you probably agree with that logic, but life has a way of knocking you down so much that you forget your inherent worth. You allow your worth to slowly erode in favor of doubt, labels, and self-judgment.

As we'll cover in different ways throughout the coming chapters, the labels and negative judgment we give to ourselves are sure to be regrets. And don't just take my word for it. The stories of people who have lived through near-death experiences present compelling evidence that negative self-labels are regrets.

There's an interesting book, *The Transformative Power of Near-Death Experiences: How the Messages of NDEs Can Positively Impact the World* by Dr. Penny Sartori and Kelly Walsh which recounts the stories of ordinary people, their near death experiences, and how that changed the course and perspective of their lives. A common theme across the stories is a return to self-love. That's not necessarily a shock, but it's an interesting anecdote to consider in the present of our lives as opposed to looking back.

When I tend to think about the end of life, I tend to picture a final judgment of sorts where all my misdeeds and failures are lined up for review. Given that, I'd expect people who lived through near-death experiences to recount how they were faced with some kind of bright light exposing all the things they did wrong in life, the things they shouldn't have done, etc. - but from the accounts in the book, that's not what happens.

The stories told time and time again by near-death experience survivors do not recount a judgment of one's life, but they do recount self-judgment. When that moment came and they almost died, they were transported to a sort of in-between for judgment. But it wasn't their actions that were judged, and it wasn't their missteps or failures. What was judged and what was deemed a regret were the self-judgments the survivors had placed on themselves in the past.

One story recounts this clearly:

"In that instant, I realized that we are all one, all connected and, contrary to common belief, there is no higher Source passing judgment on us. When our souls leave our bodies, the only judgment we endure is that which we passed on ourselves." [2]

Oof. That's heavy. When it's all said and done, the judgment we receive highlights how unkind and unfair we've been to ourselves WHILE living. It's not just a judgment of our outer lives that matters, but also our inner lives.

Take that story for what it's worth, but if that's not incentive for you to be a bit kinder to yourself with the labels and self-judgment you've been carrying around, I don't know what is.

So, let's start with the most simple but most scathing self-label we can bestow upon ourselves: "I am not enough." How do you know if you're "enough?" You might look for signs around you and you might ask yourself questions like, "Am I living my worth right now? Am I standing up for my worth? Is this decision in line with my worth?"

You might try to get specific and ask yourself, "What exactly is my worth? How much am I worth?" That's a big topic and it's not an easy one-word answer. A lot? A ton? Thiiiiiiiiiiiiiiis much?

When those answers elude us, it's easy to retreat to your space of lack once again, further solidifying the gray in your life. So, instead of trying to define these things, I recommend honing in on the very thing that prevents us from knowing our worth. And that's our inclination to think some aspect of ourselves is "NOT enough."

For some reason, it's easier in life to identify our "not enoughness" than it is to celebrate our "enoughness."

So, let's look at this in reverse order. The very thing that causes us to date people who don't prioritize us, to give away our energy needlessly to people, jobs, and friends who don't value it, to shy away from saying and doing the things that are true to us… is thinking that some aspect of us is NOT ENOUGH.

Not hot enough, not talented enough, not successful enough, not funny enough, not smart enough, not bold enough, not young enough, not old enough, etc.

When you think your body isn't enough - you convince yourself that the person who wants you one day and doesn't the next is fine - because "they want me and I'm not enough, so I'll take what I can get. Sign me up. I'm OK with hot and cold." When you think your success or talent isn't enough - you convince yourself that your boss is always right or your company is the best thing ever because you're really just an imposter and eventually you'll be discovered… so it's best to hunker down and take what you can get. When you think your personality isn't enough - you convince yourself that any friend is good enough and any attention is good enough… you get what you deserve.

Of course, all that thinking does is limit your worth and prevent you from celebrating what you do bring to the table. Everything in your life comes down to how much you think you're worth, and if you're constantly saying aspects of you are NOT ENOUGH, it's no wonder you forget that.

Frankly, I'm at war with this word "enough." Enough? Enough for what? Enough for whom? It's a ridiculous word and it's part of a ridiculous story we tell ourselves, but alas, society loves the word and here we are. Here we are defining our worth based on being arbitrarily "not enough" for other people or random standards. Here we are telling ourselves a story told through the eyes of other people.

We need to reverse this. We need to see ourselves through our own eyes for once.

We need to tell ourselves we're good enough, and THEN go out and show the world. That's the new order. It's not the other way around - hoping the world sees that we're good enough and THEN we finally tell ourselves the same. But that's how we tend to live our lives.

"A hot boyfriend or girlfriend finally means I am enough as a partner."

"Having $100K in my bank account finally means I am enough as an entrepreneur."

"Having a large friend group, receiving 1000 DMs, having headlines in the press finally means that I am enough as ____."

We need to flip the script. Tell yourself you're more than enough, and then go out and show that fact to the world. Even if you kind of doubt that fact when you say it yourself, when you go out and have a bit of wind in your sails, you're going to end up proving it. To yourself.

What would happen if you decided you wouldn't wait around for validation that you're hot enough in the form of thirsty DMs or comments or compliments? Instead, you just looked in the mirror and said, "All curves and no breaks" and then you go out into the world and prove it?

What would happen if you didn't wait for a job to promote you to finally say, "I actually am talented." Instead, you said, "I am talented," and then you just proved it with that very talent? What would happen if you didn't wait for someone to say your opinion matters? Instead, you said, "I have thoughts and perspectives that are valuable, so now listen up."

Don't wait around for people to tell you you're good enough.

Tell yourself that FIRST and then prove it to yourself with action. And the cherry on top is when other people recognize it. But the order is not what we've been thinking. The order is NOT to look outward and then inward. The order is not one, two, three like we assumed it was with self-love. Let's look inward first and then outward.

We don't do this normally. It's not in our nature. We listen first, then go inward. We wait for cues from others, and then go inward.

We look at ourselves through their eyes before looking through our own. We assume their point of view before looking at ourselves in the mirror. No more.

Tell yourself you're good enough for anything you've decided you're willing to work for, and then go out and freakin' prove it. End of story. No more waiting for proof. Decide that your definition of enough is one that is yours and yours alone and then go out and prove it.

What's an area of your life where you feel that you're falling short? Where do you feel that you're operating beneath your potential? Your career? Your inner life? Your dating life?

I'm confident that if you sit down and dive into what your definition of "enough" is for that area of your life, you'll realize it's not your definition. You've been borrowing someone else's. You've been looking at YOU through their eyes.

Look at yourself through your own eyes for once. Tell yourself a story from your point of view for once. Remind yourself that you're never less than whole while you're undergoing reinvention. Your effort defines your worth, and if you're moving in the direction of positive evolution, that can never be taken from you.

One of my favorite quotes is from author Robert Irwin: [3]

"Ever present, never twice the same.
Ever changing, never less than whole."

As you are changing, evolving, and transitioning to new versions of yourself, you are never the same and you are never less than whole. How exciting is it to affirm that? Your intention to "prove it" defines your worth, and nothing and no one can ever take it from you - no matter how many times you start over or reinvent yourself.

Your effort defines your worth. Your willingness to turn a page defines your worth. Your grace, humility, boldness, and intention define your worth. When you're proving your worth with those things, it's a healthy mix of ego and compassionate selfishness. You're out here living, loving, and viewing yourself through your own eyes.

You ignore texts from your ex because you know that their desire for you doesn't matter. You don't worry about what people think if you're an outfit repeater, a public selfie taker, a thirsty DM sender, or a brownnoser at work... because you're driven by your definition of enough.

You're not waiting for someone else to decide if you live up to their standard. You go inward first because you recognize that everything great in your life comes down to how much you believe you're worth.

You are more than "enough."

Part 3. Prove It

If you love yourself and you've decided you're enough, then it follows you "choose yourself," right? That means when you're out and about, living, loving, and working... you actually show self-love by acting on it with what you say and do.

"Choose yourself." It's the pinnacle of self-help advice and the ultimate self-improvement mantra. What does it mean to choose yourself? Choosing yourself means loving yourself AND proving it. *Emphasis on proving it*

If you truly love yourself, it's not just in theory or behind closed doors. You prove it in real life. You respect yourself, you stand up for yourself, and you prioritize being true and real to yourself with your actions. There's nothing complicated about it. You prioritize positive vibes in your life and you kick out anything or anyone who doesn't align with that. You choose yourself with your strength and your actions.

Real strength is letting people lose you instead of begging them to choose you. Real strength is choosing inner peace over "people pleasing."

Of course, in theory, we'd all live that way, right? We'd always stand up for ourselves. We'd always respect ourselves. Good vibes only, right? Well, contrary to that feel-good intention, in reality, we tend to reserve choosing ourselves for the moments AFTER bad things happen to us. After a breakup. After rejection. After enough bad, unfulfilling days add up and the frustration boils over.

Why is choosing ourselves such a backup plan in our lives? Why do we wait and wait and wait until we finally decide to choose ourselves not just in theory but finally with action?

It's because we've tried in the past.

We've all experienced choosing ourselves at some point and we learned that it can be a rocky process. It can be against us. Can you relate to this?

Maybe you were called the "bad guy" when you decided a relationship wasn't going where you wanted it? You became the "bad guy" in their narrative. Someone blamed you for their own behavior when you confronted them. That hurt. Maybe you were called a quitter for no longer wanting to always play the one up competitive game with that friend? That hurt.

Maybe you were called too ambitious when you chose Friday nights in working over going out? Or maybe the opposite - you were called a simpleton or unambitious because you appreciate a simple life and money, success, or headlines just aren't that important to you. That hurt. Maybe you were called close-minded because you prefer to date one person at a time instead of a roster and your friends called you lame? That hurt.

We've all had moments where we decided to choose ourselves with actions, and it didn't feel so great. The narrative can quickly turn on you when you choose yourself. When you prioritize yourself. When you protect your energy, your time, or your compassion. When you choose self-love.

If you've ever broken up with someone, you know it. You know you're doing the right thing, but it can turn ugly fast and you end up feeling guilty and/or selfish for doing the right thing. If you've ever quit a job, you know it. You know you're chasing your dream, you're leveling up but it can also turn ugly fast - you're selfish and a millennial job hopper. If you've ever simply decided to love yourself, focus on yourself, and DO YOU instead of being social for a bit, you know it. Your friends can turn on you. They can guilt you. You can feel the weight of FOMO.

I get that. As we've reviewed, life is about balance. Downsides are naturally attached to your superpower and to choosing yourself. What if you didn't let that balance deter you from choosing yourself all the time? What would your life look like if you decided to choose yourself 24/7? Not only when you can't take it anymore? Not only when you absolutely need to make a change?

We think that looks selfish. We think that makes us selfish, closed off, or savage. But it's really not! To choose yourself simply means you no longer hide anything.

You'd rather be misunderstood than water yourself down to fit in. You'd rather be "too picky" than settle for less than you deserve. It means you'd rather care "too much" than play it cool and ignore your intuition.

How is choosing yourself selfish? Choosing yourself requires vulnerability and, as we've covered, that's attractive.

To choose yourself means you no longer wear a mask to protect yourself from judgment. It means you no longer give away your energy unnecessarily. It means you no longer keep doors open that clearly need to be closed.

Choosing yourself doesn't need to be some grandiose gesture of closing off, cutting your hair, and moving cities. You can still be incredibly kind, compassionate, social, outgoing, and caring... and choose yourself. It simply requires acceptance that when you do... you're going to be tempted to think it's not the right move. You're going to be tempted to think that choosing yourself is not worth the cost of losing someone else or being misunderstood or labeled in a certain way. You're going to think that being called a b**** is the end of the world. You're going to think you're too much or too little. You're going to be judged - "You think you're better than me? You're faking your confidence.

Who do you think you are?" You're going to face the criticism of others and the temptation to judge and doubt yourself.

That is always always always always going to happen when you choose yourself, and I openly admit that the land of choosing yourself isn't butterflies and rainbows.

But I can tell you that every instance in my life where I finally threw in the towel and said, "I'm choosing myself"… that was without a doubt the right decision for me. Every single time. Take my hindsight for what it's worth, but I'm sure you have examples that support this in your life. They support you choosing yourself more often.

But it's so easy to talk yourself out of doing this more often because we let the criticism, judgment, and guilt that naturally accompany choosing yourself speak louder than the upside of choosing ourselves.

Let's drown out that balance with pride. Let's realize that if we can connect the dots looking back and say that any time we chose ourselves was the right move, is that enough incentive for you to choose yourself more often in the future?

The antidote to the negative feelings that accompany choosing yourself is being proud of yourself. Sounds familiar, doesn't it?

If every time you do the right thing for YOU and every time you choose yourself you simply say, "I did this and I am proud of it," there's something powerful about that. It gets easier and easier to choose yourself. Not just in the moments where you really need to. Not just in the aftermath of some BS. All day, every day.

Choosing yourself means you stop pretending that something is right for you when it's not. Choosing yourself means you stop pretending you like someone or something when you really don't.

Choosing yourself means you stop putting up with bare minimum - from other people, from your job, from yourself. Choosing yourself means you say how you feel - respectfully. It means you don't hold back because of any potential awkwardness.

Choosing yourself is how you take your power back in life. It's not by caring less. It's not by backing down. It's not by lowering the bar.

What would your life look like if you didn't treat choosing yourself as a backup plan?

What would your life look like if you didn't wait to choose yourself as a reaction? What if you did it every day? What if you woke up in the morning and you chose yourself? What if you go to bed at night and chose yourself? And in between, you remain curious, kind, and open. You're not selfish; you're not closed off. You're just real. You're real with yourself about what makes you truly happy, what doesn't, and you're real with others about the same.

When you do that, there's no need to wait until life demands you pick up the pieces and choose yourself because you're building the pieces that make sense for you.

Prove it.

CHAPTER SEVEN

Is Bigger Better?

****

*It's your story, and you get
to decide who's part of it.*

*You make eye contact first.
You laugh at your own jokes.
You take mixed signals as a NO.*

*No doubts. No drama. Anyone
who thinks you're too much for
them isn't enough for you.*

Part 1. What Do YOU Want?

Why do we want the THINGS we want in life? How did we arrive at wanting these specific things? The car, the house, the watch, the clothes, the vacation? The relationship? The adjectives we wish other people used to describe us? The timeline for success or a relationship? Heck, the definitions of "success" or "a healthy relationship" themselves?

The things we desire and the person we desire to be, as much as we might disagree, are the result of social conditioning.

Mimetic Theory is a social concept which defines the WHY behind our desires in life. The conclusion from it is that we rarely desire anything independent of the influence of other people. Our desires are largely mimetic - defined by imitating what other people want and desire. The result of mimetic desire is much deeper than wearing the same things or driving the same cars... it's formative to our identities and the labels we use to define our very being.

Mimetic Theory was first developed and studied deeply by twentieth-century French thinker, Rene Girard, and as the story goes, he developed the theory when he was young and fell in love with an amazing woman. [1] They had a great relationship, but when she approached the subject of marriage, he found himself at an emotional crossroads and was no longer so enthusiastic about continuing the relationship. He ended it, and they went their separate ways. However, what eventually drew him back to her was the fact that he saw her happily dating someone else.

It seemed that the more she wanted someone else, the more he found himself wanting her, and through this introspection, he came to realize that her relationship with someone else was modeling to him what he SHOULD want.

He wanted a relationship with her because he saw a model of it being great with someone else.

This realization set off a lightbulb moment for Girard, and over the coming decades, he found evidence of this idea of modeling throughout history, people, consumerism, and in every industry and aspect of society.

The conclusion of his writing and research is that we look almost entirely to other people for models of what we should want. It's built into the very fiber of our being, and we rarely realize it.

It's no stretch of the imagination to say that as humans we have a biological and social inclination to look for examples, inspiration, and "rightness." But Mimetic Theory says our desires in life are almost entirely social and our decisions are the result of imitating others. The theory takes the idea of "keeping up with the Joneses" but across everything we want in life and on a deeper level. [2]

There's been a lot of great writing done on this topic, and I'd recommend Girard's own writing or *Wanting* by Luke Burgis, but I offer this point about imitation to get us to the point of being incentivized to question what we want. If we've been imitating others to this point, can we push ourselves to wipe the slate clean and fill our plates with things we truly want and are genuinely attracted to - no imitation required?

Speaking of imitation, I have a sneaking suspicion that when our innermost selves have had too much imitation in our lives, something all too familiar happens - discontent, unease, and feeling lost... aka anxiousness.

There is an article in the December 2020 issue of the *American Psychological Association's Journal of Personality and Social Psychology* titled, "Normal Children Today Report More Anxiety than Child Psychiatric Patients in the 1950s." [3]

That's quite the statement - the average child today is more anxious than a child who would be institutionalized for their anxiety in the 1950s.

The studies referenced in the article showcased the result of research from children and college students, and found this to be true across the board. People (particularly adolescents) are way more anxious and stressed than in decades past.

There are, of course, many variables at play that might cause this. Maybe it has something to do with lack of community and social connectedness, higher divorce rates, or social isolation? Or maybe it's the fact that according to marketing experts, the average person sees between 4,000 and 10,000 ads every single day, and we're beaten over the head with "shoulds" at an unprecedented rate? Or maybe it's the fact that the average amount of time spent on social media per day is two hours and 27 minutes? That's a lot of comparing.

I bring up this point about anxiety within the context of desire and social influence to encourage us to consider the role imitation might play in our feelings of inner unease.

I have found the conflict between inner and outer life to be a tangible source of anxiety. That is, the conflict between what we're told to want (mimetic desire) and what our intuition is trying to tell us - THAT creates a palpable sense of unease. That's the conflict between who we are... and who we're told to be. That's the conflict between what we want... and what we're told to want. That's the conflict between the timing of our lives... and the timelines set for us.

That's the conflict between "SHOULD" and "IS." When those two things are in misalignment, it's no wonder we feel anxious. If we're hammered over and over again with examples of people who seemingly have found happiness and the "right" path for what we're told to want, it's no wonder we feel anxious. We feel anxious because things just don't feel right for us in the way they've been modeled for us, leading to thoughts like: "What if there's something wrong with me?

Why can't I find THAT version of happiness? I'm falling behind. Standing out, being different, or having a different timeline is NOT the answer."

This is just my own observation, but we'd be remiss to not consider the role mimetic desire plays in how we ended up living in the gray. We'd be remiss to not take a look at the difference between what we've been told and what our intuition wants us to consider. "SHOULD" vs. "IS."

We'd be remiss to not ask the most basic of questions: "What do YOU want?" ...not what you've been told to want... not what has been modeled for you.... not what you've been conditioned to view as "right." What do YOU want?

If you could wipe the slate clean of all the models you've been imitating, how would you answer that question?

**You deserve to trust your own timeline
instead of borrowing someone else's.
You deserve to find inner peace in
what YOU want and who YOU are.**

What do YOU want in life? Spiritually? Big picture? What do you want to do? What space do you want to take up in the world? What do you want to get out of life? What do you want to experience? A lot of the advice on this topic is centered around the Japanese concept "Ikigai" - What do you love? What are you good at? What can you be paid for? What does the world need? Find the intersection of those things and voila, you're good to go!

I also see advice that says you just need to figure out what you're willing to suffer for, and then do that. That's your thing! There's also advice that simply says, "Answer the question: 'if you knew you couldn't fail what would you do?'" Do that thing!

Those are all great answers, I suppose, and they present different approaches to this HUGE question: "What do you want in life?" But I think the simplest way to answer this is to actually rephrase it and work backwards.

Instead of asking yourself, "What do I want?" ask yourself, "What DON'T I want to regret in my life?"

This question opens the door for you to be honest with yourself in ways your inclination to imitate prevents. It's easy to delude yourself regarding what you want in life, but the topic of regret is a splash of cold water on your face. Regrets are real. Regrets are personal. I find it much easier to disingenuously answer the question, "What do I want?" than to answer the question of, "What don't I want to regret?"

Your inner honesty is what triggers a regret, and so I see regret as something that is inherently personal and that can't be borrowed from someone else. Your regrets are YOU. The real YOU. Your regrets are your "too muchness" speaking up and trying to get your attention.

Only you can be honest and say whether you'd regret something or not. So, what don't you want to regret in life?

Ask yourself this question, and I think you'll come up with some very telling answers that you can use to work backward and figure out what YOU want.

Example regrets might include:

"I don't want to regret letting go of someone I love."

"I don't want to regret staying silent."

"I don't want to regret not being more creative."

"I don't want to regret not trying."

"I don't want to regret watering myself down."

That's a solid list. Regrets have weight because of your inability to change the course of the decision that caused them. Which actions or inactions in life scare you because of their permanence?

Now, take this list and apply the inverse of those things to get a better idea of what you want.

"I don't want to regret letting go of someone I love."

The inverse of that would be something like: "I want to embrace vulnerability. I want to love confidently."

"I don't want to regret not being more creative." OK, opposite… "I want to be more creative. I want to bring my creative side to life. I want to create something."

"I don't want to regret not speaking up. I don't want to regret watering myself down." OK… "I want to be true to myself, I want to be real, I want to be honest."

What don't you want to regret? What are you afraid of not doing or not trying to accomplish? Ask yourself that, and I think the inverse will present itself as a logical intention to follow next.

"I don't want to end up in a relationship with someone who doesn't understand me." OK then, what you want is someone who understands you. That is real to you.

That is what YOU want. Maybe that's different from the example of a relationship that's been set for you?

You're better off being disappointed by the things you tried and failed than regretting the chances you never took.

Do that exercise for the different areas of your life - your career, your relationships, your friendships, and your personal self-development - your confidence, your creativity, etc.

Sometimes all you need in life is a small catalyst - a lightbulb moment that suddenly opens you up to be honest in the face of "SHOULD."

What do YOU want?

Part 2. What Impresses YOU?

To escape imitation and figure out what actually matters to YOU, I'd ask you this: What impresses you in life? What impresses you about other people? If we're sociologically wired to imitate people that impress us, this seems like a good thing to break down, right?

Let's get practical. I could easily say, "Be impressed by kindness. Don't let someone's body impress you. Be impressed by their smile." I'm not too lost in the sauce of the self-development world to know that's not very practical advice. Of course, we're all going to be at least marginally impressed by flashy things in life, and I'm fine with that. To a degree, we should be impressed by flashy things, looks, and accomplishments. Money and washboard abs will always be attractive, BUT there's a layer deeper that we should add to that.

French Philosopher Baron de Montesquieu once said:

"We receive three educations, one from our parents, one from our school masters, and one from the world. The third contradicts all that the first two teach us." [4]

I'd add a fourth to that - your own education. It likely contradicts all three. As you currently live and breathe, are you viewing the world in a way that allows you to form your own worldviews? Or are you just continuing along the easiest path? The one set by your parents, then school, and now social media and the world around you? Are you viewing people and the world with eyes that get at the truth of what matters to YOU? Not what SHOULD matter to you?

It's important to know what impresses you on a deeper level - to not live your life just floating, imitating, and hoping someone tells you what's up.

If you don't really know what impresses you, it's easy to let the next shiny, seemingly impressive thing blind you. You'll meet someone with a lot of clout or a nice blue check on Instagram and you'll be so impressed that you'll ignore the fact that they represent values you want nothing to do with. You'll meet someone who's *Forbes* 30 under 30 who has hundreds of headlines written about them and you'll be impressed by that, but you'll ignore the fact that they're really quite toxic.

What SHOULD impress you in life?

One cliche answer is: "I'm not impressed by what you do; I'm impressed by who you are," but I think it's so true. What vs. who. The models set for us… are you looking at the what or the who? The what or the why?

Think about how fast life changes. What someone has today might be gone tomorrow. What someone doesn't have today, they might have tomorrow. If you set a barometer for what impresses you as "things" - well, prepare for a wild ride. That's going to change. It's a good place to start though. You should be impressed by someone's flash, their accomplishments, their presence, etc. BUT not because of the thing… but rather the truth behind that output.

The truth behind the output - who they are, what drove them to do or be that person. The truth that drove them to be impressive... The drive behind their success… The personality that led to their fame... The work ethic that created their influence... The compassion that drove their impact…

If we're naturally going to be inspired by the people around us and we're drawn to imitate, let's figure out what is worth imitating.

It can't be the fleeting, random, and ever-changing "what"…
it has to be the "who." We have to go a layer deeper than just
the immediately impressive things in life.

**It's never too late to value
realness over big words, loud
compliments, or flashy purchases.**

Someone who's successful - OK, cool. At a glance, be
impressed. Success is impressive. Money is impressive. I'm
not trying to rewire us. But it's not the money that should
impress us - it's the drive behind it. It's the skill behind it. It's
the mentality behind it.

What impresses you? Literally just having a bunch of money?
Or the fact that this person has a drive unlike anyone else?
They worked their a** off? They believed in themselves when
no one else did? They didn't ask for permission? They aren't
afraid to try and fail?

That is the layer deeper we need to go. Because that is what is
impressive. If you take away all that money - which very well
could happen - what do you have left? Well hopefully all
those things I just listed. And those things are forever. That
drive is forever.

We have to look for the truth behind the material thing we're
naturally impressed by and are driven to model. If we're going
to model something in life, it should be something that we
can make our own - the layer behind the thing. Put their
objective impressiveness on hold for a moment. What is the
truth behind it?

You should give people two looks. You should give the
models you imitate two looks.

A first human look - that's your innate reaction to something
that sets itself apart from the norm. It could be wealth, it
could be influence, or it could be looks. It's whatever makes
them impressive or desirable at first glance.

A second look - that's where you take back your power and YOU decide if you're actually impressed or not. It's where you look to see what's a layer deeper. It's where you look to see the truth behind that thing that makes them stand out. It's where you look for the kind heart, the empathy, the depth, the creativity - the things that last and that YOU should set as models for yourself because the same elements exist inside you.

Things change - money, fame, looks. And if you're only impressed by the presence of those things, prepare for regret in the future. How would you feel if someone judged you early in your journey - before you found your groove, before you found your voice, your fame, your success, etc.? How would you feel if you weren't given a shot because you're only on chapter two of your journey? You'd say that's unfair because the person you are is there - the kindness, the drive, the creativity, the humor is there, but the output just hasn't materialized. You'd feel a bit upset about that, right? Because you know what you have to offer? It's the same when we pass judgment or imitate only based on that first look.

We need to reset what impresses us. What is the truth behind that attraction? Is it actually attractive?

If someone only has looks and no balance, no depth, no empathy…is that impressive to you? If someone only has money and no depth, no balance, no empathy… is that impressive to you? If someone only has words and no action, no depth, no empathy... is that impressive to you?

This is all rather obvious, right? But let's think about our own human behavior. A lot of the time we come to realize this, but it's AFTER giving considerable time and energy to someone or something solely because it was flashy, loud, or supported by popular opinion.

If only we had hit pause earlier and dug deeper, asked the deeper questions, and looked for deeper answers. A deeper truth. The truth behind that impressive thing. Their compassion, their empathy, their drive, their heart.

What impresses YOU?

Part 3. What Matters in Life?

All this talk about what we want, the examples set for us, and what our intuition might be trying to tell us begs the larger question: what the heck matters in life? What the heck matters!?

Life, influence, and imitation all sound pretty complicated, right? It sounds like we're just floating through life bumping into randomness, inspiration, and models to imitate all while looking inward and trying to do what's best for us. Well, ya... that's life for you. There's a lot of things trying to get our attention in life - both inwardly and outwardly.

What actually matters? I spend a lot of time considering this question because NOT having an answer to it is why I think we tend to get stressed out in life. The lack of an answer to that question is why we feel like we're falling behind, why we feel lost, and why we feel insecure.

A lot of our life's discontent doesn't boil down to the specific BS we go through, the job that treats us like trash, the people who overlook us, or the myriad of frustrating experiences thrown our way. A lot of our life's inner, soulful discontent comes from the fact that we haven't quite figured out what matters to us.

When we don't know what matters to us, we make bad decisions, we go back to an ex, we accept less in our career, and we bury aspects of ourselves in favor of the shiniest models shown to us.

If we could only figure out what matters to us, we'd also know what doesn't matter... and that is a huge breakthrough. If someone hurt us, we wouldn't let them occupy real estate in our head because we know they don't matter.

If your boss was a jerk to you, if your friend hurt you, if you embarrassed yourself, if you didn't do that thing you said you should do... AND you knew what really matters to you, you'd be much better equipped to move forward because you know what your reaction should be.

What matters to you? Here's my answer to this question. SPOILER: I'm not actually going to tell you, but I'm going to give you the keys to no longer imitating and modeling your way through life as a means of coping with the ups and downs.

What matters in life is realizing that life can be both good and bad at the same time. Life can be big and small at the same time. Life can be up and down at the same time. Life can be exciting and dull at the same time. Life can be sure and unsure at the same time.

Your happiness comes from accepting that balance. Your happiness comes from accepting that the absence of one thing in your life doesn't negate the presence of another. Your happiness comes from accepting that the absence of what you want doesn't negate the presence of what you have.

Is bigger better? Is there a right thing to want and wrong thing? Is there right and wrong timing? Is there a perfect relationship to model? A career path to replicate? I don't know. I can't answer that for you. How could I? But I do know that embracing the fact that life can be both good and bad at the same time is the key to no longer borrowing other people's definitions of right or wrong.

Life can be good and bad at the same time. Life can be clear and unclear at the same time. Life can be filled with both things we have and things we're still pursuing. Life can be filled with question marks and exclamation marks... and it can be good while those things coexist.

Recognizing this balance is at odds with how we react to the low, unclear, question mark-filled times in our lives. When things are murky and unclear, when we're just getting started, or when we feel behind or down on ourselves, we borrow and we steal. Our mimetic desire kicks into overdrive and we basically go on a stealing spree - adopting other people's desires and definitions of "right" to offset our feelings of being "wrong." We try to offset the scales to avoid sitting in that uncomfortable and uncertain balance.

We do this when we can't seem to find our groove, when we can't find momentum in our career, our dating lives, or our sense of fulfillment. When you're in that transitional space of life, you naturally feel discontent and you assume that because you're not hitting all green lights, you assume that's a clear sign that something is wrong. You're wrong. You're bad. You're falling behind. Your life will never be BIG in the way you envisioned it. And so, you turn to imitating others who seemingly have it figured out because from your view, they have it all. Their cups are filled with goodness and clarity.

But realizing that life is a balance of both good and bad, up and down, clear and unclear… and that's OK… that stops you from making those leaps in self-judgment.

You don't need anyone else's approval to be proud of progress in your life.

In the face of pressure to have everything figured out and our inclination to model people who seemingly do, I come back to the saying: "You can have it all, just not at once." In just one sentence, this breaks down the modeled expectation we've built for ourselves that says all the things you want are lying in a pile together and you need that pile! You need that pile because, look! Everyone else has their own pile. You're the only one without it.

It breaks down the expectation that to be happy you need all the things you want… all at once. Here's what I know…

You are worthy of all the things you're willing to work for, but unfortunately life is complicated. It's up and down.

There are no rules. There's no right timing. And there's no one big moment where it all clicks and you have everything you want... all at once. Rather, you get bits and pieces of the things you want and deserve throughout your life.

Life changes for the better when you realize that you 100% can have everything you want, but maybe just not all at once.

You can have that dream job. You can have that dream body. You can have that passion project. You can have that relationship. You can have that confidence. You can have that sense of fulfillment and purpose... but maybe not all at the same time.

That might sound like downer, but it should amp you up! It should make you realize that you don't need to wait anymore to be happy. You don't need to wait to be happy until that moment where everything clicks. You don't need to wait until you have clarity in every area of life.

... and you should stop assuming that the seemingly happy, successful, and fulfilled people you imitate have everything all at once. They don't.

We'll talk about comparison later in the book, but for now, know that you don't need to wait to be content in every area of life to be happy. You don't need to wait to be happy until you have everything all at once. Rather, you can and should be happy for each one as you get them.

You can have everything you want, just not all at once.

The greatest act of self-love is letting go of "supposed to be" timing and embracing your own.

When you embrace this truth, you realize that you don't need to feel guilty that you don't have those other things at the same time. You don't need to feel guilty because you haven't had that "aha moment" where it all clicks, AND you don't need to imitate in response to not having everything all at once.

You can be happy in the middle of your journey or at the beginning of restarting your journey. You can be happy when you get that job you wanted... but you're still struggling with student debt or maybe not completely happy with your body.

You can be happy when you discover a passion for making music in your living room... but you're struggling with dating and can't seem to find someone who's right for you. You can be happy when you work hard and you're in the best shape of your life... but you feel lost in your career and hate your 9-5.

You can have it all! You can have your dream job, passion, your best body, confidence, fulfillment, friends, money, etc. You can! But life isn't a straight line leading to a big pile of those things. You pick them up along the way.

Recognizing this balance sets you free. It gives you permission to be happy. It gives you permission to not model others who seemingly have it all at once.

I liken this idea to eating a fancy 5-course dinner. You get the appetizer. Then the salad. Then the main course. Then some dessert. You wouldn't eat each but wait until you're finally done and have paid the bill to say, "That was really good."

No. You would take each as they come and enjoy each. Taste it. Realize how great it is and say, "This is delicious."

We don't need to wait until we have everything we want to be happy. We can celebrate each good thing, each success as they come along. We should give ourselves permission to do this. Why?

The absence of something doesn't negate the presence of something else.

That's been the most significant breakthrough in my life. The absence of what I want doesn't negate the presence of what I have. In light of imitation and mimetic theory, that means that the absence of what you've been told to want doesn't negate the things that speak to you. Listen to that voice. Lean into it. Follow it. And while you do, don't let imitation or bad days drown it out or lead you to label yourself unfairly.

I have confidence in a far away day where my time on this fine planet comes to the end. And in that moment looking back, I'm going to realize that the good outweighed the bad in my life. I'm going to realize that all the steps I took backward paled in comparison to the steps I took forward. I'm going to realize all the things I didn't figure out are nothing in comparison to the things I did figure out.

At the end of the game, I'm going to realize that good won. Clarity won. Boldness won.

You can call me a delusional optimist, but it gives me peace and it incentivizes me to stop imitating my way through life. In the present day of your life, you're zoomed in on YOU. You're zoomed in on every step you take - every bad date, every failed relationship, every misstep at work, every failed business, every failed diet, toxic friendship, insecurity, etc... You're so zoomed in that you forget to zoom out and realize that the measure of your life is defined by the larger picture. YOUR larger picture. Not theirs.

I believe your life's larger picture will always tell a different story. Life can be both good and bad… that's what matters. Embracing that is what matters.

The absence of what you want doesn't negate the presence of what you have.

This mentality can rescue you from the gray where you're just imitating.

The larger picture reminds you that you can live an amazing life, a life filled with fulfillment and happiness and excitement and everything you want… but it's going to be alongside the lows. It's going to be dotted with steps back.

And that's OK because life can be good and bad at the same time.

PART II: BREAKING PATTERNS

To solidify what we UNLEARNED in part 1, we now must act in ways that honor our reinvention. We must pursue different or simpler. We must act in alignment with our true selves – in the face of pressure to conform.

Part 2 examines how you can bring the most vibrant, real, and bold aspects of yourself to life through the way you act and the words you use.

- Replace "better" or "more" with "different" or "simpler."

- Good things exist on the other side of embarrassment.

- Do the opposite.

- What's the best that could happen?

- Don't bite your tongue.

- It's good to feel.

CHAPTER EIGHT

Time For A Change

****

*You get back 0% of the time you
waste trying to be "normal."*

*Make that joke, be a hot mess,
triple text, eat cereal for dinner,
be a repeat outfit offender.*

*Being weird and real is what
makes your soul happy.*

Part 1. Searching For: Different or Simpler

I don't know about you, but I tend to complicate the direction of my life by thinking the key to being happy, fulfilled, confident, or whatever adjective it is I'm after - is MORE or BETTER. Maybe you do this as well? We tend to assume we need to accomplish more, do more, see more, live more, and love more in order to be happy. We think we need to chase bigger and better outcomes. And yes, while there is absolutely a time and place for that because experience is the foundation for all that life has to offer, in the pursuit of more and better, we forget that...

Sometimes a happy life isn't always about more or better. It's about different or simpler.

Now is the time to hit pause and break the cycle of always pursuing more and better and try the opposite. Now is the time to let go of beliefs, doubts, insecurities, and habits that are aligned with more and better.

There are so many habits, expectations, and timelines in life where the ONLY way we learn the lesson they have to offer us is to finally let go of them. That's the catch 22 of life. We learn by letting go. But we think we learn by holding on. We think we finally get more or better by hanging on, digging in, and staying the course. But the liberating truth of life is that when we finally decide to let go, that's when the lesson becomes clear. We need to learn to let go of the things we're forcing in the pursuit of more or better.

We need to let go of people who have already let go of us. We need to let go of the people who have made it clear that they did not choose us.

We need to let go of people who belong in our past and nothing more - people who didn't choose us, who said they couldn't make it work, or who dished up nothing but mixed signals.

Don't confuse your worth - which is more and better - with chasing it. We need to draw a boundary and let go of people who can't possibly offer more or better. Doing so opens you up to discover something different and simpler. We need to let go of people who aren't ready for us. Those are people who aren't ready to love us, support us, or have our back today - friendships, lovers, partners, business partners, etc. Don't confuse your worth with digging your heels in for someone who can't possibly offer you more or better.

We also have to turn this lens to ourselves. We need to stop looking back and saying, "I used to be stronger, happier, more energetic, etc." We shame ourselves by looking back at younger versions of ourselves as a means to lament getting older. That only further makes us dig in our heels in favor of more and better, leading us to say things like, "I've gotten this far in the pursuit of more and better. I can't stop now." Stop trying to one-up the younger version of yourself. Stop putting that pressure on yourself. Stop forcing your life to align with the "bigger and better" timelines you see online - the timeline for a relationship, buying a house, six figures, etc.

What if you chose something simpler? What if you chose something different? What if you took one month and said, "I'm going to continue to work hard, but what if I wake up each morning and said, "Today is about loving myself?" What would that look like? What if you took one month and said, "I'm going to hit pause on desperately dating and I'm going to do a 'me month?'" What would that look like? What if you took one month and kept dating, but you intentionally went out with people who were not your usual type? What would that look like?

What if you took one month and said, "I'm reserving at least one day a week to work on something I'm passionate about?" What would that look like?

Shake things up in the pursuit of something different or simpler.

I know this sounds like simple advice, but it's amazing how we overcomplicate our lives - especially in pivotal years like our 20s and 30s. As we get older, we have years and years of habits built up. We have "more and better" ingrained deep in our psyche. We have the promise of more and better at the center of everything we do from the moment we wake up until we go to sleep. More money. More confidence. More output. More outcomes. We've been cruising down a highway we built through years of not questioning if there's a different path available to us.

The only way to open yourself up to that opportunity is to say, "I'm going to hit pause on more and better and I'm going to align my vision, my actions, and my response to life with something different or simpler." Why not? Especially if you're reading this and you're saying to yourself, "Nothing is working for me. It's like Groundhog Day - I date the same people and I get the same outcomes. I work the same job. I do the same things. I'm at the same level of insecurity, doubt, or anxiety I've been at for years."

If that's you, you're a prime candidate to consider different and simpler. How can you choose different in your life? Different goals? Different people? Different perspectives? Different habits? Different places?

OR simpler? What if you took your "to do" list and radically simplified it? What if you found one thing and just focused on it this month? Instead of trying to do all things? Instead of trying to be all things?

What would happen?

The key to whatever you're looking for - happiness, success, fulfillment, inner peace, etc. - is to hit pause on more and better and consider that maybe what you deserve exists in its most complete form in something different or simpler.

Different or simpler > more or better.

Part 2. The Power of Non-Conformity

To actually embrace different or simpler in life, we have to be willing to no longer conform to pressure. We have to be willing to embrace the discomfort of non-conformity both with what we're expected to do and the conditioned habits of what we've been doing. Easier said than done...

Pressure to conform is an undeniable force in life, but the good news is that unlike the underlying psychological factor of modeling and imitating we discussed last chapter, we're more equipped to realize when we're caving to social pressure. We're more equipped to realize we're being "sheep" or falling in line to avoid feeling like an outlier.

Case in point, the Solomon Asch social experiment from the 1950s which set out to prove the tangible pressure we face to conform in life - aka "following the crowd." Asch was a psychologist whose study of peer pressure pioneered the science behind conformity, and in his most well-known experiment, he pitted unknowing participants against confederates to determine if social pressure from a large group would alter one person's behavior and decision-making. [1]

In the experiment, he filled a room with students and conducted a "vision test" instructing them to conduct a simple and obvious task - they were shown a straight line on a piece of paper and then a series of comparison lines A, B, and C. They were all then asked which of the three comparison lines was most similar to the first line shown. It was an obvious test with an easily identifiable correct answer.

He filled the room with seven confederates and one real participant who thought they were all on an even playing field. The confederates, however, were part of the research team and were instructed to answer in various incorrect ways.

Asch positioned the participant to answer last to see if the confederates' answers would influence theirs. All answers were spoken out loud.

Asch conducted variations of this test having the confederates give blatantly wrong answers, having them give a mix of right and wrong answers, and having no confederates at all to see if the real participant would conform to the majority view. Overall, 75% conformed at least once and 25% never conformed. 32% of participants conformed with the clearly wrong answers. In the control group where there were no confederates and no pressure to conform, <1% of the real participants gave wrong answers. [2]

Asch's conclusion from the experiments was clear: incorrect answers from the real participants were due to group pressure to conform. These studies were a first of their kind, and while they have faced some criticism in today's more advanced age of experimentation, the takeaway is one we can't deny: we tend to conform to popular opinion when faced with group pressure.

When asked why they gave obviously wrong answers, participants said they didn't want to be judged or thought to be "peculiar." That sounds familiar. Some participants even deluded themselves into saying they thought they gave the right answer because everyone else seemed so confident in their response. Oof.

Through various additional experiments, Asch went on to show that pressure to conform generally comes from one of two motivations: to fit in with a majority group OR to match the knowledge of the majority group because they seemingly know something not readily available to others. [3]

That sounds a lot like what we've been reviewing thus far. That's pressure to not be vulnerable, stand out, or be "too much."

That's pressure to adopt other people's goals, aspirations, and timelines because they've been modeled to us in certain "right" ways.

We, of course, know that peer pressure exists in life. Our childhoods are filled with being told to stand up for yourself, "don't do drugs," and to ask ourselves, "If everyone else is jumping off a cliff, would you?" (am I the only one whose parents constantly asked me that?) But just because we're aware we're caving to pressure, that doesn't necessarily help us avoid doing it. So, let's look at peer pressure in a new light. Let's look at pressure to conform in the light of "forcing" things in life.

When we give in to conformity, we are, in effect, forcing something. We're forcing an opinion on ourselves that isn't our own. We're forcing a timeline that doesn't align with our true timing. We're forcing dreams, goals, or expectations that don't align with our true purpose.

We suck at NOT forcing things in life. Practically, I'd say forcing things is our favorite pastime. We force relationships that don't deserve more of our time or energy. We force jobs that can't possibly offer us the fulfillment we deserve. We force friendships that are anything but reciprocal. We force interests, timelines, and put pressures on ourselves that do not align with our true talents, abilities, or timelines.

As Asch showed, conforming in the face of pressure is a defining feature of being human, and so it certainly doesn't make us bad people when we fall victim to our humanity. But how many times have you looked back on an experience and said to yourself, "I forced that. It should've ended a long time ago. Why did I keep going when I knew I needed a fresh start?"

You stayed in a relationship past its expiration date because you thought more effort and more of YOU could fill the gap between the reality of where the relationship was and the potential you so eagerly wanted it to reach?

You stayed at a job past the point of it offering you any more growth or fulfillment because you had already invested time and energy into learning the ins and outs of it? You stayed in one-sided friendships in the same way, too?

We force things in life because we think we need to. We think forcing something further - with more of us, more of our effort, more of our energy, more of our time - is the missing element. We think more is the solution to getting what we deserve in life, while deep down we know we should probably let go.

The biggest truth I've learned about NOT forcing things is realizing the thing you want so badly is not THE only piece in your life.

It's a piece of your life, but it's not your entire life.

That sentence has always been a guiding light for me - not as a way to devalue the importance of the things I want - but to remind me that life is bigger than that one thing I'm obsessing over right now. Life is bigger than success in your career. Life is bigger than love. Life is bigger than a certain timeline. Life is bigger than a certain piece of validation. The value of your life - zoomed out - is the sum of ALL those things together, not just one as it is today.

Love is an amazing part of life. It offers us purpose and connection. But it's not your entire life. Success, money, and validation through talent is an amazing part of life. It offers amazing validation through commitment and effort. But it's not your entire life.

Your body, your smile, your ability to snap necks and get thirsty DMs is an amazing (fun?) part of life. It offers confidence and connection. But it's not your entire life.

They are all important and validating, but your life's contentment comes from the sum of those pieces - not just one.

We've been given the opportunity to get life "right" in many different ways. We've been given the opportunity to find a path to happiness that includes many stops and seasons along the way. We have many pieces in life that can offer us tremendous fulfillment and happiness over time. I have no doubt that each and every one of us deserves to find the best version of each of those pieces. But we tend to lose sight of the fact that life is a series of seasons, and sometimes we go through seasons where it's not time for the love piece of the puzzle, but it is success season. Or it's not time for success, but it is time for love. Or it's not time for confidence, but it is time for fulfillment.

We tend to lose sight of the fact that we can have a season we want to be in, but that's different from the season we're actually in. When we're in forcing mode, we lose sight of that. We lose sight of the fact that life is bigger than the one singular piece. Life is bigger than that one relationship. That one job. That one timeline. Life is bigger than that one season right now. You'll get another shot at it, but right now maybe you should embrace a different season?

That one piece you want so badly is not your entire life. And if we realize that, we become willing to walk away from it if we need to. Sometimes that's exactly what we need to do - walk away today, so we can come back when the timing is right.

When you're in forcing mode, you've gotten to a point where that singular piece has become your entire life in the sense that you think your larger life success and happiness hinges on your ability to get that one piece right today. And because you've already invested time and energy into it, you double and triple down on it.

When that's the case, it's no shock you give it more and more and more and more. You force it. You force the timeline because you think your larger, zoomed out life IS that piece.

No more forcing...

You don't need to apologize for not wanting to force something - a relationship, friendship, job, or weekend plans.

I'm not encouraging you to start labeling important things in our lives as small or inconsequential. Not at all. I believe in the power of the big things - love, relationships, and commitment to ideas and effort. But sometimes we need to give ourselves the gift of thinking bigger for a moment. That's bigger in the sense of realizing that our life's summed up and zoomed out happiness and fulfillment is bigger than that one piece.

To get what you deserve, you have to be willing to let go of what is not that thing. You have to be willing to let go of who you're NOT. You have to be willing to pursue something different.

That's the paradox of life - we think that what we deserve lies on the other side of more effort and more energy. Yes, sometimes it does. But when we're in forcing mode, we have effectively closed our eyes to the fact that maybe what we deserve is entirely different.

Letting go can be the key to getting what you deserve. But it's not easy! Asch went on to conduct many more experiments around conformity and social pressure and found that the more people present around you who are pressuring you, the more conformity increases. No shock there. He also found that when the thing we're striving for is more difficult or elusive, pressure to conform also increases. Makes sense. Lastly, he found that we conform more when members of the pressure group are of a "higher social status," and so we view them as better or more influential. Been there. [4] This all makes sense, right? When we see all of social media talking about Mykonos, we think we need to go.

When we face difficult tasks, we tend to look to others for how they did it. When we see influential, rich, or attractive people tell us to do something, we jump at it.

Take the pressure off yourself. At the end of the day, isn't that why we force things in life? Pressure. Because we think we need to? Because we think we're out of options? Because we think we're falling behind? We put so much pressure on ourselves and we put so much weight and importance on certain pieces in life that we end up misconstruing a timeline, an objective, a person, or a certain season as being the entirety of our happiness.

We can't force a season we're not ready to be in. We have to give ourselves the gift of seeing the bigger picture of our lives.

Sometimes we need to celebrate a season of transition even though we want to be in a season of MORE.

We need to let go as a means of affirming our belief in ourselves. We need to let go to hang on. We have so many different shots at getting the entirety of our life right. That's the entirety of our lives' seasons. One after another as they come our way. All the pieces added up over time.

Zoom out for a moment and consider all the pieces of your life. Think about all the different ways you can and will find happiness and fulfillment. Think about all those seasons added up. Take a deep breath. Trust that path. Trust yourself. Trust your commitment to yourself. Trust that you deserve each and every one of the pieces you're working toward, but recognize that each piece, as it is today, is not your entire existence. Embrace the season you're in today.

There's a saying that says, "Nothing in nature blooms all year; be patient with yourself."

Maybe it's time to embrace that fact in a compassionate and energizing way? Maybe the best gift you can give yourself right now is stepping into a new season? A season of different? A season of simpler? That's the power of nonconformity.

CHAPTER NINE

Doing the Opposite

****

Self-care tip: *talk to yourself like your ex trying to get back together with you.*

"I'm madly in love with you."

"You're the best thing to ever happen to me."

"I can't stop thinking about how amazing you are."

"No one has ever made me as happy as you."

Part 1. Embrace the Cringe

"Embrace the cringe."

If I had a three-word mission statement for the past decade of my life, that would be it. But if we collectively had a default mission statement in our lives, it would probably be something like DON'T embarrass yourself, DON'T do anything cringey, DON'T do anything stupid. No matter what, do whatever it takes to NOT embarrass yourself. That is our natural state. Our mission is to avoid doing anything cringey because we're scared to death of embarrassment. And that aversion turns into a lifestyle where we live in the gray.

But let's back up. I'm not talking about being embarrassed because you tripped and fell in line at Starbucks, you didn't realize you weren't on mute on your Zoom call, or you got dressed in the dark and wore two different shoes. I'm not talking about life's random and unintended moments. We all have those moments.

I'm talking about moments where YOU went for it and it didn't turn out great. I'm talking about where you went in for the kiss and were denied. I'm talking about banging out selfies in a crowded gym and people giving you side eye. I'm talking about starting that podcast and having people make fun of you for it. I'm talking about wearing that loud outfit and hearing laughs behind you. That embarrassment. That cringe.

Of course, embarrassment is in the eye of the beholder, and I can try to convince you that you're only embarrassed if YOU ARE embarrassed, but you might not buy it. What you might be open to, though, is realizing that being embarrassed means something considerably more redeeming than we think.

Embarrassment is what happens when you try "too hard." Embarrassment is the epitome of embracing being "too much."

Embarrassment is what happens when you say too much, ask for too much, wear too much, push yourself too far, etc. It's what happens when you try something before you're fully ready. It's when you speak up without having a full thought. It's when you get too much confidence and it comes out in an awkward way, etc.

THAT embarrassment is a great thing! "Too much" is a good thing. I used to think that embarrassment meant lack - lack of character, lack of connection, lack of passion, lack of worth, lack of knowledge, or lack of confidence. I used to think it was a passive way of detracting from who you are and as a result, you shouldn't try because you can't lose, and you can't detract from what you already have if you don't put yourself in a position to be embarrassed.

From time to time, you will undoubtedly embarrass yourself when you try… and I'll take a life of trying any day of the week. I'd rather go fast than not at all. I'd rather put myself out there too much than not at all. I'd rather push myself out of my comfort zone than never leave it.

Embarrassing moments are simply a reflection of a life being fully lived. It's NOT a reflection of lack. It's not a reflection of not being enough or not doing enough. It's the opposite. It's a reflection that you're not sitting on the sidelines. It's you doing "too much" or being "too much."

At this point in my life, I'd rather be "too much" than apologize for being myself.

Think about how you might embarrass yourself…

You shoot your shot and get rejected. You post that selfie, and someone makes fun of you. You ask your boss for a raise, and they say that's a ridiculous thing to ask. You laugh too loudly at that restaurant, and they ask you to leave. You tell that joke at dinner, and no one laughs.

Nowhere in those equations - moments where you did something and had a cringey result - is a reflection of lack, sitting back, or riding the bench. There's no way you can say you weren't in the game. There's no way you can say you were on the sidelines. You're in the game. You're not wondering.

When your mentality is to embrace the cringe, you shift your thinking from living life on someone else's terms to your own, and the good news is we can literally train ourselves to embrace the cringe. We can practice it.

Personally, I've become competitive about embarrassing myself and it's the greatest mindset reframing I've ever done. I give myself a point for every embarrassing thing I do and I cash it in as proof that I'm in control. I cash it in for confidence - almost like winning a giant stuffed bear at a county fair. I've discovered that what you want in life lies on the other side of fear because good things happen when you push yourself "too hard" or "too early."

What you want in life lies on the other side of cringe, embarrassment, rejection, awkwardness, etc. In fact, I'd say anything worth having or fighting for in life will be found on the other side of embarrassment. I'm convinced of this.

Experiencing not so great outcomes or negative awkward feelings is a must in life because they show that you're trying. They are side effects of effort.

We have to see cringe as a side effect of boldness and positive actions - not as a symptom of lack or "not enoughness." Think about it like this...

Losing a game is a side effect of being a great athlete. Not getting a laugh is a side effect of being a great comedian. Not having a profitable month is a side effect of being a great entrepreneur. Hearing NO is a side effect of being a great salesperson.

You can't be in any of those professions without experiencing the side effects. They're going to happen along the way. There's no doubt about it.

Cringe is a side effect of living a full life. That's a full life where you're not ashamed or embarrassed to push yourself "too hard" because when you compare that to the alternative - a life where you don't push yourself at all, where you just take what's given to you, where you hope for the best and that what you want magically lands in your lap - the decision becomes clear.

To embrace the cringe, here is your mantra:

"I am not afraid to be seen."

"I am not afraid to be seen."

"I am not afraid to be seen."

"I am not afraid to be fully seen by others - whether they care or not, whether they love or hate what I have to say, whether they celebrate it or not, it doesn't matter."

Of course, what other people think matters especially if you're creating something that needs popularity - music, art, books, podcasts, etc. Of course, someone's impression of you on a first date matters.

Of course, it's great to have people enjoy your company. When I say don't be afraid to be "fully seen," I'm describing a mantra to keep you focused on what matters MORE.

What actually matters more is: trying is cool. I know that's beyond cheesy, but hear me out. Can we agree that anyone who makes fun of, judges, or shames someone who is trying... is a loser? How are you going to make fun of someone who is making an effort, who is trying something new, who is doing something personal and compassionate?

Realize that they should be the one who's judged, not you. And when that's the case, what's to stop you from stepping out and being seen? Then it only gives you two options - you step out and you're fully seen and it's great and people dig it and you feel good about it, OR you step out and someone clowns on you, but that is firmly a reflection of them being a loser.

In my life, if someone clowns on me and says, "Case, this is stupid, you're a podcaster, you're doing music, you're writing inspirational quotes on the internet?" It bounces right off me because instead of going to a place of, "Maybe they're right? Maybe I'm out of place?" I go to a place of, "Man, I feel sorry for YOU."

As long as you're not harming anyone or being hurtful with the thing you're doing or saying, I can't picture a world, where our morals, our ethics, or our humanity doesn't support the notion that trying is cool? Stepping out is cool. Doing your thing is cool.

I see someone eating dinner alone. That is cool. I see someone in downtown Chicago with a camera stand doing TikToks. That is cool. I see someone creating a podcast for the first time. That is cool. I see someone taking a million photos of their dog. That is cool. Anyone who says otherwise… that's on them and frankly, I feel sorry for them.

If I allow myself to be fully seen and it's thrown back in my face, that is on them. It really is. I don't feel sorry for myself. I feel sorry for them.

To be clear, be self-aware - don't dress up in a clown suit and then be like, "I feel sorry for anyone who laughs at me." Be practical and stay rooted in awareness, but the greatest gift you can give yourself is to be proud of yourself and anyone who tries.

**I'd rather hear NO and have
a story to tell than no story at all.**

When you allow yourself to be seen fully, when YOU judge
the people who judge you instead of yourself, you become
rooted in prioritizing how your life feels instead of how it
looks.

Start there and see what happens. Start with that reminder
and allow yourself to be fully seen. Create, start new, share,
and do whatever it is that pulls at you. Allow yourself to be
fully seen because anyone who judges that... they deserve the
judgment.

Embrace the cringe.

Part 2. Seinfeld and Opposite Day

I'm biased, but I think Seinfeld is the best comedy show that's ever been on TV. Not only do I think it's hilarious, but it also contains some hidden mindfulness gems. There's one episode in particular where Jerry Seinfeld's best friend, George, is at a frustrating crossroads in his life. He's a short, balding, pudgy, 40-something year old guy who keeps striking out in his dating life and career. He's anxious, always messing up, and consistently falling short of what he wants.

He and Jerry are talking over lunch one day, and George is voicing how frustrated he is that things never work out for him. He's about to place his usual lunch order with the waitress - tuna on toast with coffee - when he's struck by a thought.

"I always have tuna on toast. Nothing's ever worked out for me with tuna on toast. I want the complete opposite of tuna on toast. Chicken salad, on rye, untoasted... and a cup of tea." He and Jerry acknowledge that maybe that's the secret to him snapping out of his life funk. Jerry says, "If every instinct you have has been wrong, then the opposite would have to be right."

And so, George embarks on a journey where he intentionally does the opposite of what he normally does. He sees an attractive woman sitting in the cafe and has a realization that "normal George" would never walk up and talk to her. So, in the spirit of doing the opposite, he gets up, walks up to her and says, "Hi. My name is George. I'm unemployed and I live with my parents." To everyone's surprise, she's into him and they agree to go on a date. The episode then follows George on his escapades as he continues to embrace doing the opposite.

"If every instinct you have has been wrong, then the opposite would have to be right."

With Seinfeld at the helm, here we have a mindset I'd encourage you to consider. I'm not saying every decision you've ever made is wrong, I'm simply saying that if you're like most people, you're living in the gray with ingrained and unchecked habits and it's time to shake things up a bit... for the better.

What would happen if you embraced the magic of doing the opposite? What would happen if you start saying NO when you normally say YES, or YES when you would normally say NO? What would happen if you gave yourself a second chance? A reset?

Behind a strong person is a story of someone who had the courage to start over and give themselves a second chance.

We all have the most amazing but underrated ability in life - to make decisions. Every day we all have the ability to stay the course or try something new. I'd encourage you to try a 30-day challenge of doing the opposite. Over the course of 30 days as often as you can, literally challenge yourself to do the opposite of what you'd normally do or say. Be in the moment and say, "This is what I would normally do or say, so I'm going to do whatever is 180 degrees different."

Good things happen when you try the opposite! Really good things! Clarity happens! New perspective happens! Crazy opportunity materializes out of thin air! At minimum, you're going to push yourself out of your comfort zone and out of your same old habits and decisions - and that is always a good thing.

You normally go out on a Friday night? Stay in. You don't usually speak up in a meeting? Speak up. You don't usually ask for a spot at the gym. Ask for one. You never post selfies. Bang one out and post it. You're too shy to go to that salsa dance class. Sign up.

You get it. Just do the opposite of what you'd normally do. Do the opposite to prove to yourself that good things come from those exact moments. Prove to yourself that there's always something to learn about yourself and the world around you. That only happens when you start doing the opposite. It's like supercharging your personal growth. Just by doing the opposite.

This isn't LaLa Land self-help advice - doing the opposite brings diverse experiences into your life and that's been proven to provide the foundation for happiness and fulfillment.

There has been a lot of research done on the connection between new experiences, happiness, and the brain. Most recently, a study published in Nature Neuroscience titled: "Association Between Real-World Experiential Diversity and Positive Affect Relates to Hippocampal–striatal Functional Connectivity" showed that, "People feel happier when they have more variety in their daily routines - when they go to novel places and have a wider array of experiences." [1]

The researchers investigated the question, "Is diversity in humans' daily experiences associated with more positive emotional states?" Answer: YES.

The results showed that on days when people had more variability in their physical location - visiting more locations in a day and spending proportionately equitable time across these locations - they reported feeling more "happy, excited, strong, relaxed, or attentive."

They also showed that even small changes that introduce greater variability into the physical or mental routine - such as exercising at home, going on a walk around the block, taking a different route to the grocery store or pharmacy - may potentially yield similar beneficial effects. [2]

We overcomplicate life so much by thinking that BIGGER and BETTER is the key to happiness. We think that staying the course is always the key to success and happiness. But maybe it's simply doing the opposite? Maybe it's inviting more variety of experiences and perspectives into your life?

It can't hurt to at least try, right? Doing the opposite shows you what I think is the most valuable piece of life advice I ever give:

There's no right way to live your life,
BUT there is a wrong way...
and the wrong way is to
think there's a right way.

There truly is no right way to do anything in life. There's no right way to be single, there's no right way to be in a relationship, there's no right way to make a living, there's no right way to be confident, or to practice self-love. No right way. There's no blueprint for anything. How YOU live your life is how YOU live your life. How you find your realest self is how you find your realest self. You don't need to try to be like anyone else who seems to be living their truth. That's their right way. But what's your right way?

Notwithstanding things like doing your taxes, driving a car, buying a house, and other "no brainer" right ways, there is no true right way in life. How does it feel to recognize that?

You don't have to work a certain job because that's what's expected of a "successful" person. You don't have to pop bottles at the club if that's what's expected of a confident person. You don't have to be cocky and loud to be the life of the party. You don't have to meet someone on a dating app if you don't want to. You CAN meet someone on a dating app if you want to.

Those are your choices, and when you embrace your choice... that is YOUR right way.

Stay in on Friday night if you want to. Go on a two-day bender if you want (responsibly). Date if you want. Don't date if you'd rather not. Get bangs if you want. Take a week-long mental health vacation. Your confidence is your confidence. Your relationship status is your relationship status. Your happiness is your happiness.

It's up to you to define what is right for you. Maybe your happiness will come from something different? Maybe it will come from the opposite? The opposite of what you've been doing or opposite of what is expected of you? You never know unless you try.

Zig when they zag. Do the opposite of what's expected of you. Do the opposite of what you've been doing. Try something different. Drop the assumptions of what is right or wrong. There's no right way to live your life, but there's a wrong way and that's to think there's a right way.

Do the opposite.

Part 3. Murphy's Law

Don't talk yourself out of going for something different - no matter how long you've been on the course you're on, how many "Ls" you've taken, or how long you've known someone.

Can you relate to this? You're faced with something in life that's not going great, that's going slower than you'd like, that's going overtly wrong... and so you come up with the most extreme negative conclusion you can?

A couple bad dates? Getting older and still single? "I'm going to die alone." Haven't been promoted in a while? Sluggish at work? "I'm a failure." Not feeling confident, living with low self-esteem or anxiety? "I'm a loser and everyone knows."

There's something innately human that leads us to choose extremes in the assumptions we make about ourselves - especially if there's a pattern we can point to as proof (five bad dates, ten failed sales calls, etc.). It's like we internalize Murphy's Law which says that if something bad can happen, it will... to YOU. Then, when faced with a series of not-so-great life chapters, we jump to a negative conclusion. And not just any negative conclusion, but the most extreme version. On the spectrum... all the way to the left. If it can go wrong, it will.

Still single at 30? That means you're unlovable. That means you'll never find your person. If it can go wrong, it will.

Still not making six or seven figures at 30? That means you'll never be Forbes 30 under 30 or the successful person you wanted to be. If it can go wrong, it will.

Have social anxiety? That means that everyone thinks you're a weirdo, and every interaction you have is going to be awkward because of YOU. If it can go wrong, it will.

We go straight to the left side. We go straight to Murphy's Law assumption - if the bad thing is possible, it will happen to YOU.

I'm totally at war with negative and pessimistic assumptions, so here's a simple way to counter your human inclination to go to the most negative extreme. What I do is I recognize that since I tend to go to the far left on the assumption spectrum, I recognize there has to exist a far right. That's how a spectrum works, right? If there's a left side, there has to be a right side.

The left is the incredibly pessimistic assumption, but the right is the wildly optimistic and positive assumption. And I choose the right side. It's just logic. It's not pie in the sky butterflies and rainbows. It's not: "What if I fall?" "Oh, but my darling, what if you fly?" This is just logic. It's reminding yourself of another option, and then choosing it instead. Our intuition, our mind, and our soul love logic. Logic is what makes a mindset stick over a cliche.

The opposite of Murphy's Law and the opposite of, "If it can go wrong, it will go wrong" is, "If it can go right, it will go right."

I'd rather be a "hopeless optimist" than stop believing there are still good people and rewarding experiences left in the world.

Still single at 30? That means you're unlovable? That means you'll never find your person? NO! That means you dodged divorce, it means you didn't settle, it means you're about to find your person… like any day now.

Still not making that six or seven figure paycheck at 40? That means you'll never be that Forbes 40 under 40, successful person you wanted to be? No! That means you're about to break through, you're about to have your moment… like any day now.

Have social anxiety? That means everyone thinks you're a weirdo and every interaction you have is going to be awkward because of you? NO! That means your next interaction is going to be one where YOU'RE the life of the party, where you're the star and you crush it... like any day now.

Choose the opposite. Choose the right end of the spectrum. This isn't particularly earth-shattering, but I just want to encourage you to reconsider how you view potential outcomes in life. On the left is the negative assumption. The 0. But that means on the right has to be 100.

What would 100 look like in your life?

Make it up if it's not obvious to you. What's the opposite of having another bad first date? What's the opposite of flopping another presentation at work? What's the opposite of being nervous, self-conscious, or anxious? What's the 100 equivalent to the 0 assumption you've been gravitating toward? What's the opposite? Can you at least recognize that it exists?

Maybe this week will be the 100? Maybe your next sales call will be the 100? Maybe your next first date will be the 100? Maybe your next painting, your next song, or your next book will be the 100? Why not??! If it's on the menu, that means it's possible right?

Personally, when I'm in the headspace of being open to that outcome, I find myself feeling bold, motivated, and eager to try again because...

The universe rewards people who are willing to try again. The universe rewards people who are on their 10th, 15th, or 20th try.

Give yourself the fuel to try again. Give yourself the incentive to at least see what's on the menu. Don't go straight to Murphy's law assumption.

Create your own 100 assumptions and say, "If 0 is possible, then 100 is possible too."

"Anything that can go right, will go right." That's your new law.

CHAPTER TEN

Trust Me, You're Hot

****

*The most attractive thing about you is
your ability to NOT become like the
people who didn't see your worth:*

*- You compliment others when
no one is complimenting you.*

*- You listen even when
no one is listening to you.*

*- You give to others when
no one is giving to you.*

*- You're compassionate and kind when
everyone else says to be selfish and savage.*

*The most attractive thing about
you is your ability to NOT
become what has happened to you.*

Part 1. The Words We Don't Say

We have to tell people how we want to be treated. We have to speak our minds. Otherwise, we can't possibly expect anyone else to know how to truly love and appreciate us. We can't expect anyone to love and appreciate our highest color of vibrancy unless we use our words.

The words we don't say...

As we reviewed, we've gotten things so twisted in life that we're at a point where we purposely hide ourselves. We don't speak up out of fear of seeming too needy or eager. We don't say how we're really feeling out of fear of seeming insecure. We don't say what we really want out of fear of seeming too "type A" or "difficult." We don't say how we want to be treated or what we need to feel loved out of fear of seeming "too much" or "needy."

I'm sure you've had experiences in life where you spoke your mind clearly and said, "Here's what I need. Here's my real self. Here's how I'm feeling." Those were instances where you chose yourself like we reviewed in Part One. But then life kicked in, and inevitably, you came across someone who didn't understand it, who misinterpreted it, who saw it as a threat to their own needs or their own agenda. You came across someone who belittled your honesty or your needs.

And through those experiences, you THINK you learned a valuable lesson - you're better off hiding certain fundamental truths and needs. You THINK you're better off not being vulnerable because it only scares people off or is used against you. You THINK you learned a lesson that says you're better off hiding in favor of hoping to find someone who just gets you naturally, who understands you without you having to say those things.

And so here you are living in the gray saying, "Who me? No, I'm the cool, chill person. I don't need much. I'm good.

157

I'm a go with the flow kind of person"… even though you are not!

The words we don't say do us absolutely ZERO favors. Not being honest does us no favors. Pretending to be a certain way so as to not come off as needy, insecure, too confident, or too aggressive does us no favors.

You can be a kind person and still show people how you expect to be treated.

How we act shows people how we want to be treated - plain and simple. When you hold back, pretend, or hide yourself… you're telling people that you don't need more AND you're attracting those kinds of people into your life. Those people will either think you're someone you're not or they'll think you're cool with minimizing yourself.

You show people with your words how you want to be treated, and if you don't speak up and say, "Here's what I need," you're leaving your treatment up to luck and just hoping someone will just naturally know. But people suck at that. People suck at knowing what someone else needs. People can guess, people can use their past relationships to take a stab at it, but no one is the same. There you are - not being the same and having your own wants and needs - yet not voicing them.

All the while, you're thinking that will make you more lovable, but in reality, it's doing the opposite. The words we don't say literally have the opposite effect of what we think they do. We think being cool, chill, laid back, and not needing much makes us easier to be loved. But it's the opposite.

You're making the fake version of you easier to love, and in the process, you're making the real version of you harder to love.

Read that again... We think not speaking up makes it easier for other people to love us, but in reality, it just trains them that we don't have needs. And what does that do exactly? How does that serve you or someone else? How does pretending or watering yourself down serve anyone? It certainly doesn't serve you because eventually it will catch up to you. And I don't think it serves anyone else either - it's false advertising and unfair.

The words you don't say...

It's so easy for life to convince you that it's better to act like those things aren't a big deal. It's so easy for us to convince ourselves that the right person will just naturally know. But we need to recognize that honesty gets you a lot more than you think. Sure, it will 100% at some point give you the experience you fear - the experience of being honest but having it thrown in your face, having it embarrass you, or having it used against you. I wish that weren't the truth, but some people just aren't ready for it, don't want it, or see it as an opportunity to use it against you.

But even in that case, there's a powerful upside - the moment you have your honesty not respected, you now know that that person can't possibly be for you. Isn't that better than a drawn out, pretend act that eventually ends for the same reason? I sure think so. Honesty shows other people how you want to be treated. It takes the guesswork out of your needs.

A mature partner or friend will love it. Seriously. From the point of view of a mature person, what's better than being saved the time and energy of not being able to live up to what you need because you're just guessing? A mature partner or friend who wants you to be happy will love that you're guiding them to help you be happy.

Otherwise, how is someone supposed to know your boundaries unless you tell them? How is someone supposed to know what you like to hear unless you tell them?

How is someone supposed to know how you want to be loved unless you tell them? If you're not honest, you're just hoping that someone will magically know how to love you. And if you're pretending or acting, you're actively misleading them.

You're sitting there knowing that words of affirmation are genuinely important to you, but you don't want to scare them so you stay quiet. You're sitting there feeling insecure because something happened in a former relationship but you don't want to bring it up or you'll seem like damaged goods. You're sitting there saying hanging out once a week is fine, but quality time is a super important piece of validation for you so you just stew in that feeling.

The words you don't say hold you back more than the honesty you're capable of leading with. The words you don't say don't make you easier to love... they do the opposite. Speak up. Speak your mind, your insecurity, and your needs early and often.

Why do we push ourselves to be
honest with others, BUT then think
we're "too much" when we do?

I know that can be the hardest thing in the world to do because if it is thrown back in your face, it only further solidifies that fear. But let's do a quick comparison of outcomes...

Sure, be a bit patient, don't throw the whole emotional kitchen sink at someone too early, but if you're solidly in a relationship - platonically, business, or romantic - and you have important truths you haven't voiced... that person has already come to the conclusion you don't need more.

Consider your own behavior. You judge someone else's needs based on what they do and the words they use, right?

If they're always cool, chill, and acting like they're good...
you take that at face value, right? And so that becomes your
perception of them. They don't need more. "What I see is
what I get." That's human.

But what's also human, is a power move, and for the right
person exactly what they want in a partner - is honesty.
Saying, "Here's what I need." Not demanding it. Not giving
ultimatums. Simply saying, "Here I am. Here's what I've
learned I need. What do you think?" When that's your
mentality, you literally can't lose in the long term. You either
experience short-term pain in the form of someone who
either doesn't want it or who can't offer what you need. Or
you find someone who, right off the bat, gets to the core of
who you are and can offer you what you need.

Nowhere in that equation do the words you don't say serve
any purpose. The words you don't say serve no purpose other
than being a disservice to what you deserve, to the
experiences you've already been through, and the lessons you
should be holding close.

The words you don't say show people how you want to be
treated. Are you OK with not honoring what you really need?
Are you OK with a lifetime of hiding those things?

Speak up. Be bold.

Part 2. The Things We Don't Do

A couple of years ago, I saw a Tweet that said, "To be hot, you literally just have to act hot." I've been sitting on that idea for years now, and as much as that might sound cheeky and a bit disagreeable at face value, it's very true.

To be "hot" you literally just have to act hot. And I suppose by positioning attraction in this way, we are redefining what attraction really is. The way you carry yourself, the truth you emanate as you live, the qualities you lead with - THAT is what makes you hot. What you say and do is what makes you hot. It's no longer enough to be hot with just your body. To be hot is to be hot in mind, body, and soul.

Mind, body, and soul. Three things. Three areas of hotness. Three abilities.

To be hot is a numbers game, and it comes down to three boxes to check. You check two out of the three? You're hot. You check three out of three? You're hot. One out of three? Not so much. But the good news is that two of the three are completely up to you with what you say and how you act.

Mind, body, and soul. It's a combination of those things that makes you hot. It's not just "body." It can't be. If you don't think and act enthusiastically and hopefully with your mind, and if you don't live a compassionate truth with your soul... that's not enough.

Your mind... You have a hot mind when you use it. Your mind is what shows your drive, your enthusiasm, and your ability to connect with others. It's your ability to read a room. It's your ability to showcase your empathy. It's your ability to ask questions. It's your ability to get beneath the surface, to appreciate things like art, culture, and nature. It's your opinion of the world. It's your interests and your hobbies.

Frankly, it's just what shows that you're an interesting person who has an opinion about the world! It shows that there's much more to you than what someone sees on the surface. You have EQ (emotional intelligence). You can hold a conversation. You can start a conversation. You can be interested in someone else's worldview or hobbies. You have a worldview. You are curious.

That is your mind, and it's hot when you flex with it. It's hot when you make the tough decision. It's hot when you ask questions about the world around you. It's hot when you talk about your weird hobby or passion. It's hot when you are curious about the world around you or other people. It's hot when you make an effort to talk to that loner in the corner. It's hot when you're open and enthusiastic with others. It's hot when you care and show that you have an opinion that is yours and yours alone!

You know what's attractive?

Confidence to be weird and different...
An ambition to enjoy life...
Curiosity about the world...
A goofy sense of humor...

So, yes, to be hot, you just have to act hot... with your mind.

Then there's your soul... What the heck is your soul? I struggle to define it simply, but I know it's different from your mind. Your soul is your ethos. It's your perception of self. It's your gentleness. It's your willingness to be soft. It's your inner voice. It's your most aware self. It's your truest energy. It's unlike your mind which is more action oriented - what you do with your drive, with your creativity, with your money, or with your knowledge.

Your soul is literally what makes you you. It comes out in the form of a smile, a laugh, or your eyes lighting up when you see someone or something that is important to you.

It's the way you treat yourself and speak to yourself. It's the love and self-awareness you show yourself. It's the kindness you show yourself. It's the story you tell yourself and the story you tell others.

It's the grace you afford yourself when you trip and fall. It's the forgiveness you afford those who mistreat you. Is everyone out to get you? It's the gentleness with which you see the world. Is everyone else lucky and you're not? Is everyone fake? Is life unfair and you'll never get what you want? Or is there sun at the end of a storm? Does a closed door today mean an open door tomorrow? Does compassion and kindness open you up to the beauty of life? That is your soul and it's hot!

It's your ability to be kind even when someone isn't kind to you. It's your ability to love when you aren't loved. It's your ability to not become what has happened to you. It's your ability to remain soft, compassionate, and kind even when you don't receive those things yourself. It's your ability to not harden, to not lose your spark or your resolve.

Your soul empowers you to experience things in life that suck but to not turn around and become those things yourself. That is your soul, and when you use it in that way, you are hot. Your soul is what allows you to turn your back on the temptation to turn cold.

It's your ability to do the opposite. To not be loved... but to love anyway. To not be given... but to give anyway. To laugh even when no one's laughing with you. To believe in hope even though you have yet to see it come true yourself. To be optimistic even when everyone around you is anything but. To be compassionate and caring even when everyone else says to be selfish. To be bold even when you're feeling insecure.

That is your soul, and I don't know you, but I'm proud of you because I know in some way, you're living this. You've been treated in a way that you didn't deserve. You've been told you're not worthy. You've been torn down, overlooked, or forgotten. BUT whether you realize it or not, you have hung onto hope and you have not become those things yourself. That's your soul.

If you've been through a lot but refuse to let it turn you cold...

If you've found your strength through self-forgiveness...

If you've been through heartbreak but refuse to be broken...

... you deserve to be happy.

There's a reason you haven't hardened. Your softness is leading you somewhere. It's leading you to a place, a time, or a person that will reward you enormously. One day, you will look back and be grateful you stood your ground and stayed true to yourself. Amidst all the things in life you can't control and amidst all the things that frustrate you or confuse you... you made a choice not to become that way yourself. You experienced things in life that didn't recognize your worth, but you didn't turn around and treat others in the same way. You stayed true to yourself.

Your resolve to still believe in goodness will bring even more goodness and compassionate people into your life. That is your soul, and it's HOT.

At a certain point in life, we need to grow up. We have to look beyond what's on the surface. I bet you've experienced the opposite of what I'm talking about at some point. Have you ever experienced a low energy and passive soul?

Someone who's got a bangin' body and is very attractive but is very critical of the world, who is massively glass half empty, or who is only happy when they're happy and when others aren't? Someone who is attractive with their body, but who is self-centered, not empathetic, not gentle or open?

That's not enough anymore! I hope that's not enough for you, and I hope that contrast empowers you to see what about YOU really matters in the world. You have a kind, high energy, optimistic, and empathetic soul. You might not be living it 24/7 (that's what we're changing with this book), you might not be showcasing all the time because it's not easy... but you can... and when you do, that's hot.

You are attractive with your mind and soul. For all the times we judge ourselves, for all the times we feel badly that we're not hot enough or that everyone else is so much more attractive than us and we're tempted to throw our honesty in a bag and throw it out, realize that when you lean on those things with confidence... that is what makes you attractive.

You can walk in a room and be hot literally just with the way that you act. The way you carry yourself. The respect and kindness and energy you give to others. The way you live with intention and truth. The words you use, the feelings, and warmth you emanate. Here's your new mantra:

Due to personal reasons, I'm just gonna keep getting hotter, smarter, and more dedicated to my inner peace.

What makes you attractive is the warmth you radiate from your soul. It's the words and connection that come from your mind. It's the way you connect with others, the charm, the intention, the questions you ask, and the way you make someone else feel. It's the way you reflect your own passion for life, your hope for growth, and your compassion in supporting and inspiring others. You are attractive with your mind and soul.

CHAPTER ELEVEN

The Myth of Normal

****

*You have a body that moves, a heart
that loves, and a soul that dreams.*

*You exist for a reason and
you're on the right track.*

*Please keep going - the universe
will reward your persistence.*

Part 1. We're All Weird

Now that we're moving forward with a renewed enthusiasm for speaking and acting in a way that's true to us, we have to resist the temptation to think that's going to ostracize us in a permanent way. I'm sure you know what it feels like to not fit in. Maybe you moved to a new city and you felt you didn't fit in? Maybe at your job? Maybe with friends you outgrew? Maybe in your dating life? Maybe you've said to yourself, "This isn't for me. I don't get how everyone loves this or does this, but I just don't fit in."

You're certainly not alone in that experience. Everyone feels like they don't fit in at some point in life. Everyone feels like an outsider or a weirdo at some point. But we don't recognize this and we tend to see everyone else as normal and think that we're the outsider with a giant spotlight shining on us.

Why is this such a universal feeling? Why do we judge ourselves so harshly for it? Why do we think everyone else is normal and we're the outsider? Why have we become so averse to feeling like we don't fit in that we're literally willing to change ourselves to conform and avoid feeling that way again?

The reality is no one is "normal," but for some reason, we assume everyone but us is.

In fact, researchers have proven the abnormality of normal. In 2020, Yale psychologists, Avram Holmes and Lauren Patrick, published a study called, "The Myth of Optimality in Clinical Neuroscience" in an attempt to debunk the idea of normal. Through the study on both human and animal behavior and makeup, they concluded that uniformity is abnormal while variety and change among creatures is common - aka being weird or different is more normal than normal is normal. [1]

Holmes and Patrick showed that the world is NOT divided into weird and normal in any sense. They looked at a variety of traits in humans and animals and showed that they exist on a spectrum and that demonstrating a clear difference between "normal" and "weird" is generally not possible.

"I would argue that there is no fixed normal," Holmes said in an interview with ScienceDaily. [2]

There's no singular trait or quality that's defined by "normal," and if that's the case, where did this self-judgment we place on ourselves come from? Where did our barometer for "normal" come from if it doesn't truly exist?

According to Holmes, "This is a broader issue with our society. We're all striving towards some artificial, archetypal ideal, whether it's physical appearance or youthfulness or intelligence or personality. But we need to recognize the importance of variability, both in ourselves and in the people around us. Because it does serve an adaptive purpose in our lives." [3]

In layman's terms, we feel like outsiders or weirdos because we've been conditioned to believe a universal "normal" exists - some kind of optimal quality or characteristic that only you do not possess. But the reality of the research is that the only normal that exists in life is that of variability. The world isn't divided into normal and weird. It consists of variation, differences, and uniquenesses - and as we've been covering, that variance serves a purpose! Your mind, your soul, your words, and your "too muchness" all serve a purpose no matter how weird you've been conditioned to think they might be.

We're all weird in some way, but our consumption of other people's stories, media, and entertainment has led us to believe otherwise.

Of course, there are social "norms," but that's not what I'm referring to. We're also not talking about the differences that would be conditioned as clinical, medical, or psychological outliers. I'm talking about YOU. I'm talking about YOU in the inevitable instances where you feel that your interests, timelines, or traits don't align with "normal." When that's the case, let's start by realizing that it's likely a misplaced comparison against a standard that doesn't exist in the first place.

We're all weird in our own ways. but unfortunately, so many of us are unwilling to see this as a strength instead of a weakness. We all feel the limiting weight of our own unfair self-judgment. Don't put yourself in a corner by thinking you're weird and everyone else is normal. Your weirdness serves a purpose.

So, let's recognize that it's OK to feel like you don't fit in. Struggling to fit in is NOT a sign to try to fit in, it's not a sign to pretend you like something in order to fit in, and it's not a sign to retreat and slip into something a bit more comfortable (aka the gray) to try to fit in. Maybe being weird or feeling like you don't fit in is for a reason?

Maybe you're not supposed to fit in?

Maybe feeling like you don't fit in is a sign? Maybe feeling like you don't belong is a sign that you're meant for something greater or different? Maybe there's a powerful and compassionate "why" behind that feeling?

Have you ever asked God, karma, or the universe for a sign in life? Maybe you've done that when considering a career move, who to date, or a big life decision you've had to make?

"Please, give me a sign if this is right for me!"

We're all looking for signs in life to help us snap out of overthinking and make a decision. Maybe not fitting in is THE sign you've been looking for? Maybe it's a good sign?

I hope you see not fitting in as a sign of potential rather than a sign of lack. I hope you see not fitting in as a sign of redirection. Feeling weird is a sign that you're simply in a state of transition.

Just because you feel like you don't fit in and you think that's a permanent limiting factor in your life, that doesn't mean you're never going to matter, you're never going to be successful, or you're going to be alone forever.

From my experience, I am a completely different person today than I was five years ago. I'm a completely different man. I've gone from being a shy, reserved kid to having probably too much confidence. I've gone from having friends just to have friends but having no shared value sets or worldviews to having a tight group of friends who are truly ride or die. I've gone from working a corporate life but wanting something more to doing that something more.

All it took was time and seeing not fitting in as a sign that I should keep exploring what made me "too much." Had I seen feeling like an outsider as a sign to fit in, I never would have embraced the path I'm on, and that now in retrospect, PROVES that I was simply in a state of transition when I felt that way. I didn't fit in because I wasn't supposed to!

If you feel that you don't fit in, it's because you're not supposed to. I can't tell you how many people I talk to who feel and say they don't fit in, but they don't see it as a positive sign, and so they water themselves down until they fit in. They change their outlook, their wants, and their needs until they fit in and can get that nagging "I don't fit in" feeling off their back. That makes me so sad because they didn't embrace the fact that life goes like this if you just see the signs in front of you:

1. You feel like you don't fit in.

2. You realize it's OK and you listen to that feeling.

3. You end up creating where you belong instead of watering yourself down.

4. You live an incredibly real and rewarding life surrounded by like-minded people.

If we call it quits after step one, we'll never know the gift that lies beyond that feeling. I'm convinced that if you follow that feeling of "not fitting in," it will 100% lead you to people, places, jobs, and circumstances where you do fit in. It will lead you to a place and time where you're surrounded by people who support your passions and purpose and where you live vibrantly as the most bold version of yourself.

Don't let a feeling of not fitting in lead you to give up. Don't allow it to convince you that you've lost. Don't wait for the world to hand you a place where you fit in. Create it yourself. Shake things up. Change things up and create it. But most of all while you do that, remember that if you feel like you don't fit in... it's because you don't! You don't fit in! That's great. It's a good sign. It's the most redeeming sign of all.

Life gives you signs when you need them. Your intuition guides you when you need it. This is it. To think you don't fit in because there's something wrong with you is throwing away a gift. It's throwing away a lighthouse in a storm. It's throwing away a compass when you're lost in the woods.

Poetic, right? But seriously, if you don't fit in, it's because right now you're not supposed to. One day you will, and it will be so much more rewarding than watering yourself down so you do fit in right now.

While you embrace that truth, don't feel the need to be understood by everyone else.

Don't feel the need to attach yourself to any one "brand" of who you are. Allow yourself to be misunderstood.

Let people assume whatever they want about you. And be fine with it because you're rooted in who you are, in what you're about, that you don't need to fit a mold, and that you're free to be one way on Monday and another way on Tuesday. You're free to dress one way and then completely different on another day. You're free to be a lady in the streets but a freak in the sheets. Hannah in the streets, Miley in the sheets. Times New Roman in the streets, Wingdings in the sheets. INTJ in the streets, ESFP in the sheets.

It's OK to be misunderstood because you're a multi-faceted human. What they see is not all they get. What they see is their reality, not yours.

You're only "unrealistic" for someone who wants to keep you on their same level.

You're only "difficult" for someone who's always used to getting their way.

You're only "stubborn" for someone who wants your standards to be negotiable.

You're only "dramatic" for someone who is uncomfortable with honesty.

Let people think what they want. And don't feel the need to correct them. Let them assume what they want. If someone wants to think you're a boring finance bro, let them. If someone wants to think you're a space cadet floozy, let them. If someone wants to think you're a sensitive snowflake, let them. Let them because you know that's not all there is to you.

You can work hard at your finance job but also be a passionate artist. You can dress hot and look hot but you can also be an incredibly humble and talented writer.

You can be emotional and sensitive but also be incredibly impactful in your community.

Multi-faceted. If someone only sees one side of you because that's the only side they bothered to see or because that's all they had time to see... that's OK. Let them assume what they want about you. You can rest easy, smile, and feel centered in knowing there's so much more to you. Your purpose on earth is so much bigger than convincing others that you're a certain way. It's so much bigger than spending your energy correcting people. Let them assume while you actually live your truth. Your truths. The multiple facets of who you are.

If that truth is a 16-hour workday at that investment firm but when you get home, it's playing the violin, so be it. If that truth is listening to loud fist pumping house music all day but then sitting down to write poetry, so be it. If that truth is posting banging, mouth-watering selfies but then cuddling up with your partner and telling him you love him... so be it.

You're multi-faceted and you're allowed to be that way. Let them assume, but know that feeling misunderstood or like an outsider is the sign you've been looking for.

Embrace what makes you weird...

Part 2. Life on Your Own Terms

If I were to tell you to just be weird and "live life on your own terms," you might laugh at that. It sounds like a Jeep commercial or someone trying to sell you life insurance. But I'm in full support of this phrase. To live life on your own terms is to own your weirdness in the face of other people's judgment. It's to learn to give very little weight to other peoples' opinions of you. It's to draw a firm boundary between someone's opinion of you and your opinion of you. Ask yourself this:

How can anyone else's opinion of YOU hold more weight than YOUR opinion of you?

It's that realization that has supercharged my understanding that my opinion of ME always holds more weight than someone else's, and THAT is living life on your own terms.

I've never really liked binary sayings like, "No one else's opinion matters." It's not really helpful to say that ONLY your opinion of you matters. That's just not true. You've gotta be a kind and likable person in life. That's how you make friends, make connections, find your lane, your network, etc. BUT there is a difference between someone's opinion mattering and it having value.

Someone else's opinion of you matters. Your boss's opinion of you matters. That person on Bumble, their opinion matters. It matters. It exists. It's valid. Of course. BUT does it have value? Does it have MORE value than your own view of yourself? No! How could it? How could their opinion of you hold more value than your own opinion of you?

Do they know you like you know you? Do they know how you think, act, and dream? Do they know your past? Do they know the ins and outs of what you've been through?

Do they know the ups and downs of your life? Do they know what you've overcome? Do they know the ways in which you've leveled up? Do they know your inner life like you do?

No, they don't. How could they? So, in that sense, someone else's opinion of you is ALWAYS lacking in some way and therefore, it always holds less value than your own. That distinction has really helped me. Yes, their opinion of me matters, but it doesn't hold more value than my own opinion of myself. Someone's opinion of you is not your reality. It's their reality. And you live in your reality, right?

Life is so much simpler when you no longer allow their opinion of you to affect your opinion of you.

Giving more value to your opinion over others doesn't make you vain, it doesn't make you narcissistic, it doesn't make you egotistical. It makes you a realist. It makes you someone who knows your own reality and trusts that over someone else's one-dimensional assumption of who you are.

That's a powerful thing to realize when you consider how other people's opinions of you are formed. They are formed from individual moments. Those are moments where they judge you in one particular moment where you're living a certain emotion or mindset. Their opinion could be formed from a moment where you're sad, from a moment where you're frazzled, or from a moment where you're unsure or insecure. Their opinion of you is formed from their own experiences and their own reality. It always lacks the full picture of YOUR reality.

But your opinion of yourself isn't made from one or two moments. It comes from a lifetime of moments. Your opinion of yourself isn't made from THEIR reality... it's made from YOURS.

They simply do not know you like you know you. So, how can you give their opinion more weight than your own?

When you think of opinions that way, it's really tough to justify doing that, isn't it? How could they possibly understand who you are? Well, they can't, so it logically follows that if they don't know you like you know you, then how can you allow their one-dimensional opinion of you to shape your opinion of you?

Personally, I refuse to let that happen. I refuse to let someone tell me it's impossible for me to do something. They don't know me! They don't know how stubborn or driven I am. They don't know my motivation in life. I refuse to let someone tell me I need to lower my standards or that I'm being too picky. They don't know me. They don't know what I deserve. They don't know what I've learned and why I have the standards I have. I refuse to let someone tell me I'm too serious, too goofy, or too whatever. They don't know me. They don't know why I am the way I am. They don't know why I do what I do.

Sometimes people misunderstand you because they're only committed to seeing you through the lens of their own reality.

Of course, be open to other people's feedback. Be open to hearing their opinion… because it matters! It's helpful! Absolutely. New perspective can be the catalyst you need to find your groove. But it doesn't matter more than your own opinion of yourself. Because you know the full picture and they don't.

I find a lot of self-validation in realizing this and I hope you do too. It fires me up! I refuse to live an unhappy and insecure life where I'm constantly considering what other people think or what other people might think when I'm making a decision.

Instead of doing that - which is how I used to operate and how I think so many of us do automatically - now I hear their opinion and I might consider their opinion, but then I ask myself: "Is it true?" Is it true? Is what they're saying true? Is what they're assuming true?

I hear their opinion. Sometimes I appreciate it. Sometimes I consider it and sometimes I use it. But I never value it more than my own opinion of myself. That's an opinion that says, "I'm proud of myself." Or "I'm not proud of myself. I should change." THAT opinion is the one that has value because it knows the real me.

How are you going to let someone else's opinion of you supersede your own? That's an opinion from someone who doesn't know the real and full you. How are you going to let someone who rejected you change your own opinion of you? How are you going to let someone tell you that you're too much, too extra, or too eager and let that become your opinion of yourself?

How are you going to let someone tell you that what you want in life isn't realistic and that you need to think smaller and have that become your new goal? They don't know you! They don't know the real you. They don't know what you're capable of. Their opinion matters. But it's never more valuable than your own.

You're an amazing full and multi-dimensional human, and only you know all those dimensions. You're not responsible for the one-dimensional image some people have of you in their head. You're multi-faceted. But someone who only sees you twerk might think you're a total floozy. Or someone who catches you breaking a mental sweat reading the dictionary might think you're a total dweeb and a nerd. That's their opinion of you. But you know the full picture.

Your opinion of yourself and how proud you are of yourself is what matters. I hope you remember that.

Let them think what they want. Let them assume what they want. Let them tell you to be realistic, what's possible, or that your standards are too high, you're too loud, or too soft.

That's their opinion, that's their assumption based on their own reality. You don't need to have assumptions about yourself because you know the full picture about YOUR reality. You know what you've been through and what you've overcome, and you know what you're willing to do to live your best life and to be proud of yourself. They don't, and that's all that matters.

CHAPTER TWELVE

Taking Back Control

****

Look how far you've come. You've overcome the things you couldn't control and the frustrating patterns of people and circumstances. You've reminded yourself that hope is always worth holding onto.

Maybe that's the point of life? Maybe life is about getting through the hard times because you know your best days are ahead of you? Maybe life has led you to this point for a reason?

Maybe you haven't wasted any time? Maybe you're not lost? Maybe you haven't missed your shot? Maybe you're not falling behind? Maybe you're right where you're supposed to be?

Part 1. *Misogi*

Misogi. It's a Japanese word that literally translates to "water cleansing" and it describes a tradition where one cleanses their body in ice cold waterfall water. It's related to a Shinto purification ritual and it's accompanied by several other steps, a pilgrimage, prayers, or fasting with the purpose of helping one become unified with their spirit within, and *misogi* is the cleansing step. [1]

Enter a *"Misogi* Challenge." This is a modern-day challenge popularized by entrepreneur and Atlanta Hawks owner, Jesse Itzler, which describes a once-a-year enormously difficult task that you complete for the purpose of proving something to yourself, cleansing yourself of doubt, and uniting yourself with your potential.

As far as I can tell, the idea of the modern-day challenge was originally started by former Atlanta Hawks player, Kyle Korver, and spread throughout fitness and endurance sport culture through Jesse and others. It's a bit of a departure from the ritualized purification of the original Japanese term, but it retains some of the key elements. A *Misogi* Challenge is designed to help you uncover what you're capable of. It's a reminder that you're stronger than you think. In the sense of doing it yearly, it's designed to be so difficult, challenging, and eye-opening that once you complete it, it aligns you spiritually for the next 364 days until you do it again.

I've seen people do all kinds of crazy physical feats for their challenge - from running three marathons in a day to moving a rock underwater for five kilometers to continuously climbing a rock wall for 24 hours. Crazy stuff. It's taken on a life of its own, and people have applied their own lens to what type of challenges qualify as *Misogi*.

One of Korver's friends, Marcus Elliot, said, "There are just two rules: you have a fifty-percent chance of success at best, and it doesn't kill you." [2]

I don't know about that, but personally, I'm drawn to the idea of a *Misogi* challenge because it's as much internal as it is external. Its purpose is to redefine what you think is possible so that for the next 364 days, you're living with that renewed self-belief.

But what if we thought bigger? What if we lived with a "*Misogi* mindset" more than just one a year?

I know it sounds like a downer to say, "Our time living is limited." I've never really bought into the whole "YOLO," "you're gonna die," *memento mori* mindset, but as I get older, I really do see how fragile life and the human experience can be. In that sense, I love the idea of living with a *Misogi* mindset more than just once a year. That's a mindset that says... urgency.

That's a contrast to how we usually think. We're always thinking in the long term - 20 years from now, retirement, five-year plans, etc. That's great, of course, but we need to act, appreciate, and be present in the short term. Urgency. Today. Presence. We need to find ways to shake ourselves out of our comfort zones - maybe once a year with a big challenge or maybe once a week with small but intentional *Misogi* challenges.

That's something I can certainly get behind - intentionally putting yourself in situations that challenge you, and not just because of mindsets like "no pain, no gain," but because the more you embrace the things we're literally wired to have aversion to - radical honesty, awkwardness, rejection, embarrassment, first steps, starting over, etc. - the more we come to harness the power of those very things.

As we've reviewed, the greatest moments in life and the greatest first steps you can take are inevitably going to be amidst times that require courage and vulnerability.

The idea of a *"Misogi* mindset" can be just what you need to push through. It can inspire you to DO. To act today. It can be used to inspire action right now - to embrace a challenge and to redefine what is possible for you time and time again. *Misogi. Misogi. Misogi.*

When you're in the moment and you're afraid that being honest with someone might make you look "crazy" or "too much." Do it. *Misogi.* When you're about to give a sales pitch and you're nervous about failing. Embrace it. *Misogi.* When you're looking for a new job, interviewing, pitching your music or art. Go for it. *Misogi.* Redefine what's possible for yourself. That's *Misogi.*

Here are your new mantras:

Some of my life's best days haven't happened yet.

A bad day doesn't erase the progress I've made.

I'm proud of how much I've changed.

I've come too far to be talked out of what I deserve.

I'm no longer scared of asking for more.

I love the concept of going all out once a year in the hardest way possible. If you can find a way to do that and do it in a big physical way, great… go for it. But I like this idea even more for living it frequently. A *Misogi* mindset. Today. Tomorrow. And the next day.

That's a mindset that says you can redefine what's possible for you each time you step forward and embrace the challenge. And you can do that weekly, or even daily. A *Misogi* mindset says that if it scares you, you HAVE to try it.

Great things exist on the other side of fear, right?

But life certainly isn't that easy and it'd be ignorant for me to say, "Just do it."

Fear of rejection, conditioned fear, trauma, and fear in general can be quite personal and debilitating to the point where "suck it up" just isn't practical or effective advice.

So, I can't just try to amp you up blindly. But I can give you a mindset you can keep in your back pocket. The next time BEFORE you talk yourself out of trying something new, before you retreat to your comfort zone, you say *Misogi*. Before you come up with reasons why you can't, you say *Misogi*.

Misogi recognizes that the things that scare you are the most rewarding. There's no way around it. The things that make you feel nervous or unsure, they're the most rewarding - from starting a business to shooting your shot, to asking for a raise, to standing up for yourself, to creating something personal. Those things are always always always accompanied by fear and uncertainty. How could they not be?

The good things, the life-changing things, the things you deserve - they will always be accompanied by something you need to overcome. They will always redefine what you previously thought was possible. We usually come to realize that fact, but it's only after we've let it pass us by dozens of times, or only after we've given up, or after we've lowered our standards. But *Misogi* says the more challenging something is and the more it scares you, then you must do it. *Misogi* gives you urgency and willingness in the present.

Obviously, we've strayed pretty far from the original idea of ritual purification, but I do think there's a deep soul element here as well. When you identify that thing you need to do whether it's daily, weekly or yearly, there's power in that decision because inherently, it's personal. It's FOR you. It's about you. It's not about anyone else. It's not about fitting in. It's not about appearing a certain way to someone else. It's about you.

Regardless of the outcome of your effort, THAT will always be a superpower. That's your ability, for once in your life, to separate what is expected of you from what is true to you. That's your ability to separate pressure to be "normal" from embracing being "too much."

That's powerful. *Misogi* says: "This is for me. Other people might not understand it, other people might judge and ridicule it, but this is for me."

THAT'S the real power of this idea. It describes your ability to separate what you've been told from what you want. It's your ability to separate being "realistic" from being true to yourself. It's your ability to separate their expectations and their timelines from the ones that make the most sense to you. It's the ability to embrace your boldness. That is what *Misogi* represents.

Keep this word and its redefining power in your back pocket. The next time you're tempted to talk yourself out of something because it challenges you deeply, or it opens you up to failure, disappointment, or rejection… before you retreat and start listing all the reasons why not… say *Misogi*.

Misogi means you redefine what is possible for you each time you're willing to try.

Part 2. What Makes YOU Happy?

I want to put a thought out there: maybe we've been going about the things we want in life backwards? We say we want happiness. We say we want inner peace. Love. Success. Fulfillment. It's great to want those things and pursue them in life through effort. But maybe we've been going about the process backwards?

"It is not happiness that brings us gratitude, it is gratitude that brings us happiness." [3]

I'm drawn to this quote for the conclusion I take from it when it comes to the process or the order of things in life. It reminds me of PEMDAS. Good ol' order of operations. What do you do first to get your answer? Parenthesis, exponents, multiplication, division… There's a certain order to do things in math and science to get you to the result you need.

The beautiful thing about life is there is no right way to really do anything. There's no right path, there's no blueprint, and there's no five-step plan, but there's something to be said about the order of effort. The order of your vision. The order of outcomes. While there might not be a right path for anything in life, there is a certain practicality we can turn to that challenges us to try a different order.

In the case of, "It is not happiness that brings us gratitude, it is gratitude that brings us happiness," maybe the result of the goal is what we should try to get in the first place? Whoa…

We think that happiness makes us grateful, but maybe gratitude is what will make us happy?

If your goal is to be happy, how have you been going about this goal?

Have you been doing what so many of us do - saying, "I'll be grateful when I'm happy.

I'll be content and at peace when I'm happy. I'll smile when I'm happy. I'll take time to appreciate what I have when I'm finally happy?"

Do you fall into the human trap of setting a finish line without considering that the things you think exist there are actually the things that will help you get there in the first place?

I, of course, don't know what it takes to be universally happy, but I do know the idea of switching things up might be just what you need to break through.

You're not missing out when you decide you have everything you need to be happy.

Maybe happiness is about being grateful? Maybe it's not happiness that makes us grateful? Maybe it's the other way around?

If that's the case for happiness, maybe we can get practical about life in other senses too? What are some of the goals you have for yourself? You want to be loved? You want to be successful? You want to be confident? What are the assumptions you've made - that perhaps in a moment of vulnerability - can be revealed to be backwards?

We want to be loved and we think a relationship will give us that and make us love ourselves... Well, maybe it's not a relationship that makes us feel loved, but rather it's loving ourselves that brings us a relationship?

We want to be successful and we think a paycheck is proof of that... Well, maybe it's not a paycheck that makes us feel that label of successful, but rather it's being "successful" by our own definition that brings us a paycheck?

We want to be confident and we think being liked by others is proof of that...

Well, maybe it's not being liked by others that makes you feel confident, but rather it's being confident that makes people like you and be drawn to you?

I recognize I'm just throwing around words, but it's the order here that should get us thinking. What if we've been chasing one thing - being loved, being successful, being confident - and we've set finish lines there hoping that checking that box will give us the side effects of that goal, but all along it's the side effects that will help us get to that goal?

In the instance of wanting to be loved, a relationship is certainly part of being loved, but is that THE path to loving yourself? Well, certainly in a sense, but what if you switched it up? What if you loved yourself first and saw what happened?

Practically, I can tell you for a fact that in dating, you can sense when someone loves themselves or whether they are filling a void by looking for a relationship. No one is a bad person for that, of course, but loving yourself is a huge step towards actually finding the partner who's right for you. Loving yourself makes you confident, gives you a strong sense of self, shows what you bring to the table... and that shows in dating.

In the instance of wanting to be successful, that's a vague subject and everyone's definition of success is different, but I'd venture to say that most of our definitions include some reference to a paycheck or financial freedom. That's great, but what if we're so focused on needing certain dollar amounts to finally feel worthy of the "successful" label that we miss the fact that success is what breeds money, not the other way around. What if we focused more on our hard and soft skills knowing the paycheck will come from that effort? What if the practice and the craft will make us worthy of that label, not the paycheck itself?

Personally, I've earned more in my career as a result of leaving behind guaranteed paychecks that on paper fit the bill for the successful label. I've earned more by investing in the things I'm good at, taking risks, and letting them lead me to my definition of success.

And confidence... this one we all have backwards. We think confidence is this thing we get when we've conquered our demons and we no longer care what people think of us because we're just walking confidence magnets and people are drawn to us. Sure that's a part of it, but maybe it's not being liked by others that makes you feel confident and worthy? Maybe it's confidence that makes people be drawn to you? Maybe confidence doesn't come from "the result" - people liking you? Maybe it comes from reps? Experience? Failure?

I truly don't know the path to the big goals we have for ourselves, but I do know that sometimes we have things backwards. We look at the little things - gratitude, being present, self-love, being liked by others, etc. - and we think those little rewards come from the big things - a relationship, success, confidence.

Ask yourself: What would be the side effect of the big thing you want in life? What would being loved by someone give you? What would being successful or confident give you? You might say inner peace, lack of pressure, gratitude, presence...

Well, what if you tried those side effects FIRST instead of waiting for the big thing to give you them?

Having a partner, having nice things, and having confidence certainly will give you the means to take a step back and focus on those smaller things, but what if you tried them first? What if you did subtraction first? What if you looked your fifth-grade math teacher in the face and defied those parentheses and did multiplication first?

What if you stopped being desperate for a partner and stopped overthinking failed relationships and love? What if you stopped pressuring yourself, and instead loved yourself so much that it emanated from you in everything you do? Perhaps your next first date would be your last because you're so centered in yourself that you're undeniably attractive and a total catch?

What if you stopped pressuring yourself to measure success by a paycheck or title, and instead, you went all in on a skill or talent, and you showed it to the world, you showed it to your boss or your company, and you just saw what happened?

What if you stopped wanting everyone to like you and you stopped looking at other peoples' reaction to you as a sign of your confidence and instead you TRIED to fail, you embraced embarrassment, you embraced self-awareness as much as possible, and you see what confidence THAT gives you?

What if we tried the little things TODAY that we think will be given to us TOMORROW as a result of getting that big thing? What if we practiced gratitude today and see how happy that makes us? What if we practiced radical self-love today and see how that affects our dating lives? What if we embraced failure and awkwardness and see how that boosts our self-confidence? Why not?

What makes YOU happy?

Part 3. Please, Keep Feeling

You're doing better than you think. You're doing better than you're giving yourself credit for. I genuinely mean it.

Quick story - I dated a girl in my mid 20s and she was great. Truly. But one of the misaligned qualities that probably had something to do with us breaking up was the fact that she lacked curiosity (a VERY important quality to me). For instance, we'd be chatting about something random and a question would come up such as, "What's the capital of Spain?" Or something even more random like, "I wonder what time the Chicago Museum of Contemporary Art opens?" or, "Is the legal drinking age 18 in Europe?"

Without fail she'd say, "Oh well, I dunno" and would move on with her life. She would just leave the question there and I was always left wondering, "How can you just move on?! Don't you want to know?"

I know that's such a small thing, but I'd say when faced with a simple question and an even simpler way to find the answer, most people would pull out their phone and find out quickly. You have a question, a curiosity, or something that's easy to find out, most people take quick action to get the answer.

To me, if you have a curiosity and an easy and immediately accessible way to figure out the answer, why wouldn't you? Why would you leave that question mark unanswered? Why wouldn't you give yourself that little win? That little new fact or that new understanding?

It, of course, doesn't make anyone a bad person if they simply don't care. I'm sure in some instances I've said, "I don't care to know more. I don't really need that piece of information." It's very situational, and there are things I certainly don't care to take even five seconds to do.

But I give this example as a means to show you the idea of cause and effect in life. You have a question and so you work to find an answer? Cause and effect.

You are doing better than you think because you still listen to the cause and effect in your life. You have a question and you work to answer it. You laugh when something is funny. You cry when something is sad. You get food when you're hungry. You speak up because you have something to say. You try something new because you're bored. You ask for more because you deserve it.

Cause and effect. That might sound obvious and you might be thinking "Duh, Case… that sounds like being human. Stimulus and reaction."

Well, yes and no. I've been podcasting and writing about human behavior for the past eight years and I've talked to hundreds, maybe even thousands of people. I've heard countless stories of growth, failure, rejection, life, love, work, career, and everything in between. And something I've found to be incredibly common as people age is that a lot of people give up on reacting to life. They have the cause or the stimulus, but they just stop reacting to it. They turn passive.

They adopt what I referenced in Chapter One - an "it is what it is" mentality. That's a defeatist mentality. That's a numb mentality. That's a mentality that says, "What's the point? What's the point of trying? What's the point of chasing curiosity? What's the point of trying something new?"

"What's the point of looking up the answer if I just have another question?"

"What's the point of being excited if I'm just gonna be hurt?"

"What's the point of starting a new project if I'm just gonna fail?"

I don't know if that's you and I love you either way, but you're doing better than you think because you're still hanging onto cause and effect in your life - in big ways or small ways. You haven't given up. You're doing better than you think because you're still living with cause and effect. That's your human, compassionate, curious, bold, and driven cause and effect.

You tell someone you love them because you love them. You start a new project simply because it excites you. You go to a movie alone because you want to see it. You're willing to go on another first date because you still believe in what you deserve. You see goodness in other people because you still believe in positive intent. You try a new food dish because you saw it on TikTok.

You're doing better than you think because at the end of the day, you're active. You're not passive to the cause and effect in your life. You're at the center of your own universe and you haven't given up and just said, "It is what it is."

"Between stimulus and response there is a space. In that space is our power to choose our response. In our response lies our growth and our freedom." (Viktor Frankl) [4]

If you're living your life - no matter your age, status, life stage, etc. - and you still chase curiosity, you do what interests you, you say what's on your mind, you're willing to speak up, you're willing to try something new, you're OK with being a beginner again, you laugh when something is funny, you cry when something is sad, you go to therapy, you're inspired by life around you… then you're doing better than you think.

You don't need an outcome in mind, and there's no "win" necessary, you just do what your heart tells you to do. You follow what your human inclination tells you to do. You don't turn it off because life has gotten you down.

You're doing better than you think because the alternative is very very real. That's a life where you just say, "What's the point? I'm this way, I'm this thing, I've had this result before, so what's the point of new, more, or different?"

Living life in that way is NOT the life you deserve. You have so much more to get out of life, you have so much hope and compassion in the present and future, and if you're living with the cause and effect in your life... well, then you're doing better than you think.

Even if you've been in a funk and you're half-way in with "what's the point," the good news is that you can revitalize your life. All you have to do is give into the compassionate cause and effect in your life. All you have to do is listen to the deep, human, and personal part of yourself and start acting on it again.

If something makes you curious, look it up. If you have a question, ask. If a part of you wants connection, fun, or excitement, text a friend even if it's been a while. If you think someone is attractive, tell them. If you want to try a new hobby, start it.

Cause and effect. That's the small cause and effect in your life that you can control quickly and immediately.

Give yourself a 30 second rule to really amp things up. Act on that thing in 30 seconds. Push yourself to un-numb yourself. Push yourself to be anything but passive. Be bold. Combine that with the opposite challenge we reviewed in Chapter Nine.

See what happens. Giving into cause and effect will give you more shots in life. But more than that, doing this will show you that in the face of statements like, "It is what it is," well, it's actually NOT. It's not, "It is what it is"... it's what YOU decide it is.

And if it interests YOU, if it makes YOU curious, if YOU want to try it, if YOU want to say something… YOU do it.

You don't let your curiosity take a back seat. No! You're alive! You have an intuition that gives you hints about what's best for you. And the best way to reinvigorate your sense of self is to listen to yourself again… in small ways. And small ways become big new chapters.

Stay curious.

CHAPTER THIRTEEN

New Beginnings

****

There's nothing wrong with choosing what makes YOU happy.

You are NOT defined by a title, relationship status, or someone else's timeline.

It's a gift to live your life where you're cool with being alone but also cool with falling in love.

You're just living your life but open to the day when someone comes along and amplifies the happiness you already have.

Maybe you've found this person? Maybe you haven't? But either way, it's OK to choose what makes YOU happy and to prioritize finding love within yourself.

Part 1. The Power of Contrast

Life gets better because of your past, not despite it. Life gets better because of your past, not despite it. Life gets better because of your past, not despite it.

The opposite of what we want - the breakups, the sadness, the anxiousness, the failure, the rejection...The contrast in life is what makes the things we want and deserve so rewarding.

I understand that those experiences objectively suck. Once we've heard so many NOs, once we've been through several "failed" relationships or worked a draining job for so long, it's tempting to just say, "I just want to skip past the BS and get to the result." Of course, we want to avoid those things and get to the good part. But here we are living in reality and so inevitably, we find ourselves face to face with the literal opposite of what we want.

Maybe there's value in that contrast? Maybe we can take the lessons and move forward with hope and confidence? Maybe we can find the energy to try again even if it's for the 50th time? Maybe we can live with hope and optimism even if we feel beat up and the last thing we want to do is try again or start over?

Contrast is what makes what we want so rewarding in life.

You want to be with your soulmate, right? Let's be honest - if you actually skipped past all the BS in life - all the bad first dates, all the five-month long relationships that never made it, or the brutal long-term breakups along the way - would the outcome of finally being with your soulmate be as sweet? I don't think so.

What makes finally finding your soulmate and being comforted by their permanence and compatibility is the contrast from your past.

What makes finally finding your soulmate so rewarding is the impermanence and lack of compatibility you experienced in past relationships. Contrast is what makes the things we want rewarding. In fact, I think contrast is the catalyst for actually helping us define the things we want.

We want a partner who has a sense of humor... because we've experienced someone who didn't. We want a person who understands us... because we've experienced someone who doesn't. We want a job that is rewarding... because we've experienced a job that isn't.

We all have inherent ideals of what we want in life, but those are all theories until we've lived the opposite. So, maybe there's *some* value in contrast after all? And certainly, acknowledging this doesn't make frustration, heartbreak, or lack of fulfillment any less draining. But it reminds you that that outcome you seek is the outcome you seek because of contrast. Past contrast is what makes the things we're working toward so rewarding and worth the wait.

**Life gets better because
of the past, not despite it.**

What makes something worth the wait? Well, I think it's the fact that ideally once you have that thing, it's forever and it's the best version of it that you can possibly imagine. What makes it the best version of that thing you can imagine? The contrast! The times where it wasn't forever. The times where it very clearly wasn't the best version.

The next time you're presented with a frustrating outcome, where you've gotta pick everything up and start over, where you were close but no cigar, where you were hopeful but ended up frustrated and so you've gotta go back to the basics - relationship, dating, friendships, career, your creativity, talent, entrepreneurship, etc. - consider the value of the contrast you've been presented with.

You didn't choose it and you wish it weren't the case, but you're here now. With contrast. With the opposite of what you wanted. Can you look at it and say, "This is going to make the moment I get that thing so much sweeter?" Can you look at it and say, "This contrast further solidifies what I deserve?" Can you believe that life gets better because of the past not despite it?

I think this is a life-changing mindset. The ability to look at outcomes that disappoint, times where you've gotta pick up all the pieces, put them back together, start over, and say, "This sucks, but this contrast is going to make the outcome I want AND deserve so much more rewarding when I get it" - that is powerful!

Can you find upside in the contrast in your life? Can you find the upside of the people who hurt you? Maybe you can find healing there? Maybe through this healing lens you can recognize what the people who hurt you gave you?

**Healing is not allowing a past chapter
to be the end of your story.**

**Healing is deciding the universe has
something better in store for you.**

**Healing is no longer accepting crumbs
because you deserve the whole bakery.**

**Healing is forgiving yourself for thinking
what you've been offered is what you deserve.**

The people who hurt you are the ones who show you what you deserve. Recognizing that is not giving them credit. We're not in any way thankful to the people who hurt us, betrayed us, or frustrated us. We're not victim-blaming ourselves or anything like that. We're simply recognizing that the contrast from people in your life solidified your worth, your standards, your sense of self, and your centeredness.

The people who betrayed you, disappointed you, rejected you, overlooked you, or misjudged you reminded you of your worth.

Think about a life where you always get your way, where all you hear is YES, where people jump to support you, where you get everything you want, and where you're never hurt or rejected. If that was your life, how would you ever know what it means to stand up for yourself, to make a tough decision, to say NO, to spot a red flag and leave, etc.? I don't see how you would.

The people who hurt you by saying one thing and doing another, the people who ghosted you, who betrayed you, who broke promises... What did that hurt give you? It showed you what you deserve.

You deserve someone who doesn't lie, who is real with their words, and who has true intentions. You deserve people who support you and don't have ulterior motives. You deserve respect from the people you work with. You deserve communication from friends and partners. And although the opposite of those things suck, after the fact, your worth is no longer just theory. It was proven by the contrast.

There's value in that contrast because it's one thing to run down the usual checklist of things you deserve and not really think twice. It's one thing to read this very book and say, "Yes, I deserve what Case is talking about." It's another thing to live through the direct opposite of those things.

That is how a standard becomes real and permanent in your life. Contrast did that.

Looking back at those instances of contrast, there's a powerful lesson in having put yourself in that vulnerable position in the first place. To be hurt, you dropped your guard. To be hurt, you connected with someone. To be hurt, you let that person in. To be hurt, you tried.

To be hurt by someone means you trusted yourself enough to be vulnerable and open up. You were willing to be first to try or first to be vulnerable. And even though that was ultimately thrown back in your face, it's a powerful truth about you. It says something about who you are. You were willing to connect, trust, and be hurt.

Think about a time when you were hurt by someone. Maybe it was dating and someone led you on but never had any intention for more and ditched you? Maybe it was the way a long-term relationship ended? Maybe it was in your career and you were never listened to or never appreciated? Maybe it was with your family and your effort was never enough or you never felt your parents were proud of you?

Now fast forward to today. Consider the things you do - the habits and practices you live that speak to your worth. You stand up for yourself. You speak up when you have something to say. You disagree with someone when you know they're wrong. You act on your intention when you get a bad vibe from someone. You call someone out when they're being disingenuous. You're willing to say NO. You ask for something you want.

How do you think those practices came about? You didn't just wake up and start doing those things one random day.

You do those things and you'll continue to do them because the people who hurt you reminded you of your worth and now it's real to you.

The pain ultimately subsided but the reminder stayed. That's what contrast gives you.

**You are entering a new chapter where
you meet the proof that your
standards were never too high.**

Now you stand up for yourself, you say NO, you refuse to get drawn into toxic relationships, you express your worth in what you do and say and wear, and you practice your passions and hobbies as boldly and vibrantly as you want.

Now you live your worth and you recognize the path to get here hurt, but your standards and sense of self can never be taken from you.

That's the power of contrast.

Part 2. What Are You Bringing With You?

Let's talk about bringing those standards and sense of worth with you along your journey - no matter how winding the path is. I've come to realize that the people who end up creating the most fulfilling, rewarding, and happy lives for themselves are those who are willing to start over as many times as needed. Those are people who see starting over as an opportunity rather than a reflection of loss.

Life gets better when you decide you can reinvent yourself as many times as you need.

Undoubtedly, in the pursuit of being your truest, brightest, and boldest self... you're going to have to start over. We've been reviewing various ways to stop conforming, to do the opposite, and start fresh - and that's going to require quite a few fresh starts and periods of reinvention.

But for some reason, we tend to think of hitting restart as a reflection of failure. We see it as a reflection of messing up so badly that you need to start over from scratch. We see it as a reflection that we're throwing away something. We see it as a reflection that we've emptied the proverbial bank account and we're going to start from zero.

But being willing to start over is the key to breaking through! Now is a good time to turn to our mantra: "A happy life isn't always about more or better; it's about different or simpler." A willingness to start over is the key to embracing a different and simpler life.

I'm sure you've heard the self-help soundbite: "When you start over, you're not starting from zero, you're not starting from scratch... you're starting over from experience." Like most people, I used to throw that aside with a dramatic eye roll.

"I invested two years in this relationship and now I'm starting over. How is that not zero? How is that not starting from scratch?"

"I gave that job everything I had for five years. How is getting another job not starting from scratch?"

Well, let's remind ourselves of the concept of "points" that we reviewed in Chapter Nine. Those "awkward points" describe your ability to do something awkward, challenging, embarrassing, out of your comfort zone... and each time you do, you get an awkward point. And eventually you keep doing that and you're like, "Wow! I have 50 points," and you cash that in for confidence because your confidence was built through the experiences that showed you those things didn't change you at all - they didn't change your worth, rejection didn't change you, embarrassment didn't change you. Through those experiences, you created confidence for yourself.

Those points add up, and the scary, awkward, vulnerable experiences that came from them gave you the foundation for the mentality you want - confidence, self-worth, higher standards, etc. It's the same exact mentality when it comes to starting over. When you decide to start over, you're taking all the points you accrued up to that point and you're bringing them with you. When you start over, you're not starting from zero. You're not leaving those points behind. You're bringing them with you.

Starting over isn't about what you're leaving behind, it's about what you're bringing with you.

When that's the case, how can you look at starting over as throwing something away or starting from zero? You're not. You're building on top of what you already created. You're moving closer to cashing in those points.

Sure, there might be a period there where you feel like you're at the beginning because you've gotta do a lot of the crap that's associated with starting over and yes, that's true. But from a mindset perspective... you're the furthest thing from zero.

Starting over is you saying: "I can't cash those experiences in here. I can't cash these points in for happiness with this person. I can't cash them in for success and fulfillment with this job. I can't cash them in for confidence with these habits. I can't cash them in for happiness here in this place. BUT I can move to another place, another person, another job, or another habit and cash them in there. I'm bringing them with me."

Starting over is less about what you leave behind, and so much more about what you bring with you. You're never starting from scratch. You're never starting from zero. You're always always always starting from experience. You just have to be willing to end that chapter.

It's as the saying goes: "Beginnings always hide themselves in endings."

Those experiences might have been frustrating, you might feel like you invested too much time and energy into something and now ran into a brick wall, but keeping your head up and having eagerness about a new beginning is what reminds you of what you're bringing with you.

No bad ending can take that from you. No breakup can take that from you. No toxic work environment can take that from you. No disappointment can take that from you.

You're taking those tickets with you. Those tickets are the lessons you learned, the standards you've established, the things you learned about yourself, and the boundaries you've set. Those things CANNOT be taken from you!

What you take from chapter two, six, or ten carries into the next chapter. What you take from relationship one carries into relationship five. What you take from job three carries into job five. And when we realize that, starting over becomes less daunting. Sure, it's still difficult. Getting back into dating, moving cities, starting a new job, doing a new workout... Yes, that's tough.

Why are we afraid to start over when every time we have, we've come back stronger, smarter, and more attractive?

But once you say, "It's OK to start over," it's a lot easier to actually do it. It becomes so much easier to take that first step because you see it as moving you closer to what you deserve rather than further away from it. That's what happens when you remind yourself of what you're bringing with you rather than what you're leaving behind.

It's the next step. It's the next chapter. It's you taking everything you have with you from the last step, the last chapter, and bringing it with you. And when that's the case, there's no zero. There's no shame. There's none of that. Starting over is just the next step.

Wouldn't you rather start over today than continue to hold onto points that you can't possibly cash in? If you knew you couldn't find happiness, success, worthiness, or self-love in one place... wouldn't you move on to another place? Wouldn't you move on knowing you've already done a lot of the work and you're so close to cashing in?

You're not going back to zero when you start over. You're starting from experience. You're starting from a standard. You're starting from what you know is good for you, from what grows you, from what loves you. You're bringing a lot of greatness with you! You're bringing everything you've built, all the work you've put in, all the lessons you've learned.

That's a lot of points. And it's the opposite of what we tend to think.

We think that starting over means we have to build up our reputation all over again at that job. It means we have to play 20 questions on first dates until we're blue in the face. We have to make new friends in a new city. And yes, those might be true. That's reality. But you can stomach that so much easier if you know that you're not starting over with your worth, with your experience, with your standards intact.

You're not starting a new job and you're all of a sudden entry level with no understanding of the business world. Heck no... you're bringing with you all the deals you've closed, the projects you've led, the management experience you have. Those tickets are all yours, and it's only a matter of time until that's rewarded.

You're not starting dating without any understanding of what you want or need. Heck no! You're bringing with you a thorough understanding of what you need, the red flags, and so on. It's only a matter of time until that's rewarded.

Starting over means you're moving closer to what you deserve... not away from it.

Starting over is the necessary next step because you can't cash those things in staying where you are. You can't cash those experiences in there. You can't cash those standards, that skillset, that self-love in there.

You simply need a new environment to explore.

And there's no shame in that because look at what you're bringing with you. Seriously. Look at it. That's a lot! It certainly is not zero. And that's what starting over is all about. It's not about what you're leaving behind, it's about what you're bringing with you. What are you bringing with you?

PART III: NO GOING BACK

To embrace our boldest selves, we must stop comparing ourselves from a place of lack and we must start trusting our intuition.

The last part of this book helps you resist the all too familiar human feelings of self-doubt, imposter syndrome, and the temptation to return to what is comfortable.

- Comparison is THE source of discontent.

- No more "people pleasing."

- Have no expectations, but high standards.

- Respect the feeling, but don't invite it in.

- There are NO coincidences in life.

- Loneliness can be a strength.

CHAPTER FOURTEEN

Comparison, the Thief of Joy

****

*I'm sure you get this all the time,
but you're the perfect combination
of mind, soul, and body.*

*You're a radiant disco ball of energy.
You're a part-time unicorn, part-time human.
With each passing day, you're smarter, funnier,
and more dazzling. Please don't forget that.*

Part 1. Instagram Vs. Reality

According to some studies, as much as ten percent of our thoughts involve comparisons of some kind. [1]

We spend 10% of our brain power comparing ourselves to others? WHAT?! If that doesn't freak you out, I don't know what will. Comparing ourselves is THE source of discontent in our lives. It's what leads us to rush, lower our standards to avoid feeling behind, and be unfairly judgmental of ourselves.

You've made it this far in the book, and we've reviewed quite a few ways for you to reinvent yourself in the face of pressure to conform, conditioned habits, and false expectations. At this point in our journey, do you agree with the following statement?:

How others see you is not as important as how you see yourself.

In Chapter Eleven, we reviewed why someone else's opinion of you is always lacking in some way, so I'm hoping you're at least willing to say YES to some degree. If that's the case, can you carry that logic further and say, "How I see others is not as important as how I see myself?"

"How I see others is not as important as how I see myself."

That specific missing belief is what causes us to compare ourselves from a place of lack and give away our power. It's what causes discontent in our inner lives. It's what causes us to overthink and feel like we're falling behind.

It's great to be inspired by others and it's great to find examples of people you think are good role models. I'm talking about the negative kind of comparison that says people with dates on Valentine's Day are happier than you are.

I'm talking about the negative kind of comparison that says a hot person on Instagram is inherently happier than you. I'm talking about the inner turmoil you dish up for yourself when you assume someone else is happier than you because of some assumed perception of them - their looks, their photos, their friends, their confidence, etc. I'm talking about the kind of comparison that leads you to have thoughts like, "They have the right way and I have the wrong way." That's comparison from a place of lack, and it needs to stop.

What a weird way to live life! That's saying you are less than someone else or beneath them because of some perceived lack. But let's splash some water on our faces and realize something: there is no way whatsoever to truly know if someone else is happier or fulfilled. You truly do not know. Social media is not real life. Their perfect lives and their perfect posts are not real life.

To think someone looks more attractive than you, more influential than you, or funnier than you, and as a result, has a menu of unlimited fulfilling things they do all the time with an exciting life from start to finish... it's just not true. Here is your new mantra:

**"I'm too busy doing my own thing
to compare myself to others."**

We're all searching for the same things in life no matter what is shown on the surface. And while you are still searching and you're doing it alone or on a different timetable... it's easy to compare and assume YOU are lacking. But it's not true. Case in point, an experiment I did on Instagram in early 2022. At the time of the experiment, I had around 440K Instagram followers, and I posted a question for anyone to answer.

I asked, "What's missing from your life?" and I got thousands of answers. Adventure, sleep, romance, happiness, purpose, friends, money, confidence, motivation, peace, travel, calm, rest, vacation, direction, real love, financial security, clarity, confidence, consistency, hope.

Those are deep answers, right? Big things! Big rewarding things that you probably also want, right? Big rewarding things you assume people who seem happy, attractive, and successful already have, right?

I posted that question, waited for answers, and then I clicked through hundreds of accounts to see WHO posted each answer because I wanted to see if MY perception of them based on their Instagram profile aligned with THEIR reality: the answer they gave.

Someone said "financial security" is missing from his life. I clicked his profile, and it was a man whose feed was filled with pictures of friends in fun places, on vacation, playing paintball, traveling, with cars, and at the casino in Vegas. This guy seemed like he was living a financially-free life.

Someone said "having true friends" was missing from her life. I clicked her profile, and it was a woman who had a ton of pictures on her feed with friends going out, on vacation, at bars, etc. This woman seemed like she had more than enough true friends.

Someone said "direction" was missing from his life. I clicked his profile, and it was a guy speaking on a stage at a conference and who posted thought leadership and inspirational quotes. This guy seemed like he had plenty of direction in his life.

Someone said "deep love" or romance was missing from her life. I clicked the profile and this woman was a 10/10. As the stereotype goes, you'd think she'd have potential partners lining up to be with her. She seemed like she had plenty of deep love options in her life.

Reality vs. the surface. On the surface, it's easy to compare yourself to those types of people and assume that you are the one who lacks. They SEEM like they lack nothing. They are attractive, successful looking, outgoing, and their social media solidifies that narrative. You assume they have countless lovers at their fingertips, they always have things to do, trips to go on, a huge friend circle, they have full bank accounts and are just happy, fulfilled people who are never lonely or lost.

But by their own admission in my experiment, you can see they still lack things in life. They are still in search of the very things you are also in search of.

It's easy to compare yourself from a place of lack because of the weight we give social media. But what can bring us back and empower us to stay in our lane is to realize that everyone is still searching for the same things in life. No matter how they look, what they've done, who they are, or how many friends they have... no one is perfect. Social media is not real. What you see on the surface isn't the whole story. How could it be?

We are on OUR own journey just as everyone else is on THEIR own journeys... but we're quick to forget that because we do this very human thing where we assume that anyone who looks attractive, successful, or happy on the surface has it all figured out and is 100% happy.

We're all on our own unique journey, and I find solace in remembering this and not ostracizing myself by thinking I'm the only person on a journey of discovery. I find solace in the German word *sonder* and what it's come to represent. Author John Koenig describes this term in his book, *The Dictionary of Obscure Sorrows*, where he describes specific emotions or feelings that have no English words. [2]

SONDER (noun): The profound feeling of
realizing that everyone, including strangers
passing in the street, has a life as complex
as one's own, which they are constantly living
despite one's personal lack of awareness of it.

We're all on the same journey despite not realizing it. Feel like you're the only one who's lost or unsure? "It's not true."

Say that the next time you're tempted to say, "Why am I not them? They have it all." It's not true. See how that rewires your self-judgment. Maybe that small realization is what you need to be a bit more kind to yourself and also confident in YOUR timing and what YOU are doing.

What you think of yourself matters more than what someone thinks of you AND what you think of yourself matters more than what you think of others. We have to reframe once we hit the point of seeing what THEY have as a reflection of our own lack. We have to reframe once we hit the point of seeing their "perfect" Instagram post as a reflection of how we are falling behind in life. We have to reframe once we hit the point of seeing their hot selfie as a reflection of our lack of sex appeal. We have to reframe once we hit the point of seeing their vacation in Bali as a reflection of our lack of success.

Come back to this logic: how you see yourself is more important than how you see others. See their success and their 10/10 looks, their dates, and their edited pics on Instagram, but know their gain doesn't mean your lack. Their happiness doesn't mean you're miserable.

You might be saying, "Case, it's not like that. I don't think less of myself. I know deep down I want what they have, I know I'll get it, but I'm frustrated because I want it today. It keeps eluding me, I'm tired of waiting and falling behind." I get that, but it's the same story: what you think of yourself matters more than what you think of them.

Yes, that's couple goals. Yes, you want that success. Yes, their confidence is admirable. But reframe that to what YOU think of you. "Yes, that's couple goals and that's confidence... I'm excited for that milestone in my life. I'm building my confidence. Soon."

"Yes, I want that success and I'll have it soon because I'm working my a** off."

"Yes, that confidence is admirable and I'm working towards loving myself and soon it'll be mine."

You'll have it. You'll be it. But in the interim, their gain is not your loss.

You look happier since you stopped letting social media rush you through life.

Let's take back our power. Let's take back our power by realizing that when we compare, we lose twice.

When you compare yourself to someone else, you lose twice. You lose first when you decide that someone else's way of living is the ONLY right way and you need to copy that to be happy. And you lose a second time when you decide you're less, you're beneath them, or you're falling behind when you don't have what they have today.

You lose twice. But you don't have to lose at all.

And that's by reminding yourself that what you think of you matters more than what you think of them. Override that human inclination that we all have. Sure, be impressed, be inspired. Great. But turn back to you. Look inward. Remind yourself of what you have to look forward to. Remind yourself of what you're creating for yourself. And that you'll have it.

If you'll have it soon, why does it matter if they have something you want today?

Why does it matter if they have it today and you'll have it tomorrow? Why does it matter if their today is your tomorrow? Why should their today affect your today?

Your opinion of you is what matters. Remember that the pressure you put on yourself is not yours to carry. Stay in your lane, believe in what you deserve, and follow the logic.

Your opinion of YOU is more important than their opinion of you. AND your opinion of you is more important than your opinion of them.

Part 2. Perpetual People Pleasers

"The Perpetual People Pleasers" sounds like a great band name, but really it's a description of who we've become. We make decisions out of fear of letting other people down. We do our best to avoid disappointing people. But to free ourselves from negative comparison, we have to be willing to let other people down in life. We have to be willing to disappoint other people. We have to put an end to being people pleasers.

It's OK to let someone else down in life. In fact, I think if you're not disappointing some people in your life… you're not living a life that is true to you.

Showing up for yourself means choosing inner peace over "people pleasing."

As we've reviewed, change is a requirement for growth. Change is what happens when you start being true to yourself. Your taste in romantic partners changes. Your choice in friends changes. Your goals change. Your vision for your career changes. The way you perceive yourself changes. Your standards, boundaries, confidence, and worldview all change as you grow. It's a requirement for growth.

And inevitably, those changes are going to alter your relationships. You're going to find yourself moving away from certain people and toward others. You're going to find yourself saying NO when you used to say YES. To be bold, you have to be willing to let go of people, habits, experiences, and places that no longer support the realest version of yourself. To be bold, you have to change.

If you allow those changes to happen, you're going to disappoint some people. But if you're a perpetual people pleaser and you're living a mentality that says, "I don't want to let anyone down," you're literally blocking those changes.

Because inherent in growth is letting people down who no longer fit your vision for life. It must happen!

We need to disappoint some people. Doing that gives you receipts - proof that you're growing. "Show me the receipts. Receipts or it didn't happen."

If you're not letting people down occasionally in your life, I don't see proof of the changes you're making in your life. I'm not encouraging you to be "savage." I'm not suggesting you become a person who lives with reckless abandon - canceling plans, becoming flakey, ghosting other people, or getting a face tattoo just to disappoint your mom. I'm simply encouraging you to give yourself permission to disappoint others when you have to. You're allowed to let other people down.

That can take so many forms - it could be the simplest example of going on a date with someone, not feeling the vibe, and simply saying, "I'm not sure we're a match." And that person could be super sad as a result. They were feeling you. But you didn't vibe with them. They're going to be disappointed. If you wanted to, you could lead them on and try to ghost them or let it die in the hopes of letting them down easy to avoid disappointing them overtly. That's the easy path, but it's the path that blocks your growth. OR you could be compassionate to them and yourself and just let them down. Rip the bandaid off. It's done.

We outgrow friendships all the time. It happens. It's life. You can embrace that however you like, but don't beat yourself up for no longer wanting to booze it up with the old college crew or hang with work colleagues who only want to gossip. If that doesn't fit the future you want for yourself, it's OK to disappoint them.

If you find yourself saying, "I don't want to disappoint them, so I'll keep saying YES," as minor as that might seem, you are literally getting in your own way.

You are blocking the change you need to be embracing. You are not respecting what you want and what you deserve.

This isn't carte blanche to go nuts with "bye, Felicia." Be thoughtful. Respect people who have been there for you and have supported you. But I find it freeing to realize that when I make a decision that someone isn't meant to be part of my journey anymore… It also means I'm not meant to be part of theirs any longer. And that helps me realize that it's actually compassionate both ways.

"They're not part of my journey anymore… and I'm not part of theirs."

It goes both ways. You've outgrown them or they've outgrown you. Either way it's OK, because you're both changing. You need that change. They need that change. It's compassionate to both you and them.

This year we're allowing ourselves to outgrow the things and people that are no longer for us.

You can care about the opinions of others. You're going to. You're human. But there's power in recognizing that you don't exist to please everyone. You're not on this earth to make everyone love you and support you. You don't exist to make everyone happy. If you did, what would that mean for your growth? That would mean you're not in charge of your own growth. But life doesn't work that way.

Life is about making positive changes in your own life that fulfill your innermost and honest realizations and at the same time, being compassionate to others in the process.

If you're getting in your own way, that's not going to happen. As weird as it might sound, when I let someone else down because my expectations of myself don't align with their expectations of me - I'm proud of myself.

Because right in front of me - even if it's awkward or a bit painful - I have proof. I have receipts of my growth. There's no greater reflection of your personal growth, your career growth, or your maturity in relationships than compassionately letting someone down.

We're human and we're wired to not want disappointment or awkwardness. But remember this - some people are not meant to be a permanent part of your journey, and you're not meant to be a permanent part of theirs. It goes both ways. You're allowed to change just as they're allowed to change.

No one else knows what's best for you. No one! Not that guru. Not that influencer. Not even your parents. Only you. So, you have to set yourself free from the pressure we all have to please everyone and let no one down.

It's OK to say goodbye. It's OK to let go. It's OK to disappoint. It's the only true way to respect your trust and your potential. I don't see it as a negative reflection of you. Be compassionate. Be direct. Be honest. Be bold. But know that it's necessary. Those receipts mean you're growing.

It's OK to let someone else down in life.

Part 3. Table for One, Please

The noise in life… The commentary from the peanut gallery. The assumptions other people make about you. The things your ex said about you. The words your coworkers use to describe you. That thing that person said to you on *Hinge*.

That's all noise, and you have the ability to let it affect how you see yourself, the person you are, and the things you think you need to do… or it can just be noise. To embrace our real selves in the face of temptation to compare ourselves to others, we have to learn what is noise and what is truth. We have to learn to realize that we can rely on ourselves.

You can rely on yourself.

I don't say that in the sense that you don't need anyone in your life, that you shouldn't listen to others, or that you're just gonna ride solo forever. The subtext to all this is that you should be compassionate toward yourself but also openly invite people into your life that complement it. BUT while you're looking for those people - friends, lovers, business partners, strangers on the internet, etc. - it's so important to realize that you can rely on yourself.

You prove this to yourself in moments where someone tells you you're too needy. You're too sensitive. You're asking for too much. You're asking for too much in a partner. You're asking for too much in your career. You're weird for having a certain hobby or interest in a topic. You're weird for having a certain dream or aspiration. You're too much. You're too quiet.

It's all about how you react to THAT noise. Your answer should be, "That's cool. Thanks for your opinion, but I'm good. I can rely on myself."

No one knows you like you do. No one knows who you are on a deep and soulful level.

No one knows WHY you have the understanding of the world you do. No one knows why you came to have a goal, a dream, a standard, or a boundary.

Most people you'll encounter in your life - with the exception of family and lifelong friends or partners - are hopping in on a random page or a random chapter in your life. YOU are living each day, each page, each chapter, but they're just hopping in on a random day.

That person you met on a dating app - you've lived 29 chapters before they meet you at chapter 30. Your new boss at work - you've lived 20 chapters before they meet you at chapter 21. That new friend, that business partner, that person on the internet - they're meeting you at a random time on a long timeline of events and chapters you've already gone through.

And all those chapters you've already lived…. only you know them. Those are chapters that taught you aspects about yourself, who you are, what you want, what you deserve that only you know. Those are chapters that are close to your heart. They are part of you, who you've become, and who you're becoming. Those people simply have no idea. So, the noise they create… it's irrelevant. It's not informed. Only you know the truth, the past, the foundation, the WHY, and because of that, you CAN rely on yourself.

Behind a strong person is a story of someone who said, "I deserve better" and never looked back.

How does it feel to know that on your worst days, on the days where you feel you're falling behind, on the days where you're told you're too overeager or too needy, you can say, "I can rely on myself. This is just noise. It's their noise. It's their noise that knows nothing about me."

You're dating someone and they start saying things like, "You're too direct or eager… what's up with that?" You can, of course, listen and hear them out… but only you know WHY you're that way. Only you know what happened on chapter 24 in your life that led you this way. Only you know why you've grown to speak up for yourself and what you want. Only you know the relationship and interactions you had in the past that shaped you. They don't.

Or you're told that, "Your passion for something is silly. Your passion for standup comedy isn't going anywhere." They think you're goofy or you try too hard or whatever. You can hear that feedback but rely on yourself. Because only YOU know why you have the passion.

Only you know that making other people smile and laugh is something near and dear to your heart - that you made a promise to your grandmother when she was about to pass away that you'd make her proud, that you'd make others smile just as she has made you smile. People don't know that. People don't know your why, your past, the chapters that shaped you.

You can hear noise, but you can still stand centered in knowing that you can rely on yourself. You can rely on WHY you are the way you are and, of course, be open to change and evolve, but foundationally… you never have to doubt yourself or allow that noise to tear you down.

That commentary is their commentary, and it doesn't serve a purpose in growing you. If someone wants to label you a certain way, have at it. If someone wants to say you're too loud, let them. They don't know. They don't know your "why." They will judge you from the lens of their own reality.

If someone wants to say your standards are too high and that you're a "grass is greener" person, let them. They don't know. They don't know your "why."

They don't know that you didn't used to have a very high opinion of yourself. They don't know that you lost yourself in that process and you used to allow people to take advantage of you. But then you did the inner work, you created confidence, and now you're living it and you refuse to go back to being that passive person. So, let them make their commentary. You know your WHY and you know your growth.

If someone wants to say you're weird and your art, music, or inspirational quotes are immature, let them. They don't know YOU. They don't know that you never felt talented and that you never felt that you had anything to offer the world. But then you found your voice, you found your talent, you found your creative side, and it showed you that you have a voice, that you matter, and that you have a talent and impact. So, let them make their commentary. You know your WHY, you know your growth.

Life gets better when you decide being weird, different, or eccentric is your superpower.

Doesn't that feel good? You know your full story. They simply do not. It's great to let people in. It's great to be vulnerable. But far too often, we let strangers, acquaintances, coworkers, or random dates into our lives and we allow them to make us feel a certain way - guilty, weird, too much, too little, etc. But they simply don't know! How could they?

You CAN rely on yourself. You have the power of choice. You have the ability to filter out what someone says. You have the ability to be a kind person and say, "NO, thank you." You have the ability to choose what you allow into your head and heart.

You have the ability to differentiate between the things you absorb as truths and the things you define as noise.

"That's just noise. That's their commentary, that's their noise... that's them walking in on a random chapter in my life."

You can rely on yourself. You can rely on your understanding of yourself and find peace and calm in appreciating who you are and what you've become.

Of course, balance this with an eagerness to continue to evolve and to not let your past shape your future. You have the present and future to continue to work, build, and change... but in the meantime, control the noise: do you allow other people to change your view of yourself?

You can allow someone to convince you that you ARE indeed too loud, too needy, your standards are too high, you're a freakin' weirdo... OR you can assign their commentary to your junk folder. Straight to spam.

You can rely on yourself. And the people who you do want to get to know you, the people who you invite into your life on a deeper level... that's great... but everyone else... "I can rely on myself."

That first date on Hinge who refuses to understand you. That colleague who thinks you're overeager. That friend of a friend who thinks you're weird. That stranger on the internet who says your content is stupid. That cousin who says you're too much. Let them be.

You can rely on yourself.

CHAPTER FIFTEEN

Got Standards?

****

*In case no one told you today,
high standards look amazing on you.*

*You should be proud of yourself for
holding onto them even when it's
easier to lower the bar.*

Part 1. Picky or Selective?

As you step into your most vibrant and bold self and never look back, you're going to need new standards and boundaries to match this new version of YOU. Those are standards and boundaries that are firm, non-negotiable, and demand the same love, compassion, energy, and effort you put forth.

As you start to live them, you might be tempted, however, to think to yourself, "Am I being too picky? Am I passing up on people or experiences that are meant for me?" You might hear people say, "Who do you think you are? You're too needy!"

If that's you, consider this: Are you being "too picky" or are you just being selective?

There's a difference between the two, and with a bit of introspection, you'll realize you're selective and that's the best quality about you. It's something to never let go of and it's something to never doubt.

You're not missing out on anything when you're busy upgrading yourself and your standards.

You, my friend, are selective. You are selective in who you give your time and energy to, who you date, and who you do business with. Being selective means you know what you want. It means you know what you deserve. It means you don't jump at the first thing that smiles at you. It means you're building standards from experience because you have proof of WHY you should have those standards. And that's different from being "picky."

Being picky is version 1.0 of having standards and it's a good thing, but it's just the starting point.

It started in the gray - you didn't exactly know what you wanted and deserved, but you're in touch with yourself and you knew you should set standards that respect who you are. You were unsure what that looked like specifically, but you knew you should have high standards. So you might have borrowed them from other people, or had a blanket sense of, "I have high standards."

Being selective is version 2.0, and it means you've lived through the opposite of what you deserve and now you're rooted in knowing WHY you'll never go back. Being selective means you're open to anything and anyone but you're not going to do any chasing. Being selective means your past is powerful. It means you've lived and learned, and now you have proof for WHY behind each standard.

Being "picky" is passive energy. It means you have standards but you don't really know what they are specifically or why you have them. You just know that you're supposed to protect and respect yourself. That's 1.0. Those standards are what you're told to want or look for.

You're 2.0 now. That means you've seen, touched, and learned first hand, and because of that, you have a personal WHY behind each standard you live. You have proof. You know why you have high standards for honesty, communication, respect, openness, hard work, motivation, worldviews, ethics, morals, etc. - ya know, the things you've lived through the opposite of.

So, to answer the question, "Am I too picky?" Heck no!

You're not being picky anymore; you've leveled up past that and now you're selective. You're selective because of the proof you have in life of why you should have a standard or boundary.

Real strength is turning a scar into an unbreakable new standard.

If you're doubting yourself and thinking you're too picky or you're holding yourself back too much, ask yourself this: "Is there something in my past that taught me to have a high standard?"

Yes? There's an ex, an experience, or something in your past that taught you to have a higher standard? That's all you need to know. You're not picky. You're selective because you have proof. You're selective because you have a WHY.

When you're selective, you have a centered and powerful understanding of what you deserve. It's no longer good enough for someone to rise to meet your standards. You're selective, and that means you're going to wait until someone is there in the first place. They meet your standards in who they are and what they do. There's no need to rise up. They're already there because they've done the work just like you have.

Version 1.0 of you said, "I know I deserve to live with high standards. I'm not quite sure what that looks like, but I'll know when I find it." Version 2.0 of you says, "I've found it. I've experienced enough BS to know how I don't want to feel. I have proof of what I deserve because I've been through the opposite."

You've upgraded to selective and you shouldn't forget it now that you're embracing your boldest self. Don't throw it out the window when it changes your timeline or makes you uncomfortable in the face of "easy" paths or the "usual" type of people.

The reality of life is that there are a lot of cool, nice, and "good enough" people, places, and circumstances out there. And that's great news! But the even better news is that the most rewarding and long-lasting people and experiences are on the other side of being selective.

That's you being selective because you have experiences that taught you to be this way.

Selective means you know there are people out there who are already at your level. There are people who meet your standards and you meet theirs. Because of that, you know it's OK to be selective in every area of life - dating, friendships, work, career, creativity, etc.

Being selective is built on experience. It's built on what you've been through. It's built on what you've learned. It's built on recognizing how valuable your energy is. It's built on recognizing that the most powerful mentality you can have is one where your expectation of someone isn't that they rise up to meet your standard, it's that they are already there. And same with you. You're already there.

In the case of who you give your energy to - there is someone who exists that will not have to rise to your standard because they're already there. There is someone with whom you can create together… not chase. There are people and experiences that are worth being patient for.

You started out being picky and that was the starting point, but now you've leveled up and you're selective. You're like the final boss. There's no going back. There's no going back to what you've been through. Look your doubts in the eye - "What if I'm being too picky? What if I'm needlessly throwing away people and experiences?" - and say, "No. I'm not being too picky. I am selective and I deserve someone who is the same."

You're never asking for too much when your standards are built on experience. You're never asking for too much when they're built on knowing what you deserve because you've lived through the opposite. You're never asking for too much when your standard is simply a standard of reciprocity.

There's no going back. You're not asking for too much because you recognize that life, love, and everything in between - yes, it comes with tradeoffs, no one and nothing is perfect, and you're going to have to fight through the ups and downs - but you're never misguided to operate from a standard of being selective.

Speaking from personal experience, when you have high standards, you probably find yourself frustrated when they're not met. You match with someone on a dating app and you're excited... BUT then you meet them and they fall short. You get a new job and you can't wait to start... BUT then you get there and it's a toxic work culture and you realize it was a huge mistake. You expect your friends to be there for you and to support you... BUT when they fall short, you think to yourself, "I have the worst friends in the world. FML."

Simply put, you get frustrated when your expectations aren't met. So what should you do? As crazy as it sounds, I recommend replacing the high expectations you have for yourself and the world around you with no expectations at all.

No expectations, but high standards.

In place of expectations, have high standards. Your high standards will remind you that you can handle anything, and that's way more valuable than having high expectations for outcomes. Your high standards will get you the outcomes you desire. The moment you realize your worth is not valued, someone isn't going to step up, or a certain circumstance is beneath you… you turn to your standards to redeem yourself. High standards are what rescue you from being tempted to think your life sucks or you're missing out.

Your standards say you won't continue to hang out with people who disappoint you. Your standards say you won't date someone who doesn't choose you. Your standards say you leave a job that is toxic. Your standards say you find new friends if your old ones don't grow with you.

High standards > high expectations

I'm not suggesting you live a life with low expectations because there's certainly a difference between having low expectations and no expectations. Having low expectations would mean the bar is so incredibly low that the smallest thing would qualify as "enough" for you. Someone holds the door open for you? You'd fall in love with them. Your job gives you an extra day of PTO? Best job ever!

None of that. Simply have no expectations for outcomes in the present. You're not accepting defeat. You're simply replacing high expectations with high standards, and this shift in mindset takes you from hoping, wishing, and waiting... to a mindset of, "Whatever happens happens, but I'll be fine because I know what I bring to the table and I'll make the right next move." This is the epitome of the healthy side of your ego we talked about previously.

Having no expectations but high standards frees you from tying expectations to any "right" path. It frees you from attachment to outcomes. You're not expecting the worst from people or circumstances - you're simply no longer projecting an expectation.

You know what you deserve, what you bring to the table, and you welcome new experiences and people into your life. And now you view everything through the lens of your standards rather than high expectations. There's no self-blame. There's no, "My life sucks; all I get is bad luck," etc. All there is is knowing that your standards dictate what you do next.

You are entering a new chapter where you meet the proof that your standards were never too high.

You hear NO? "That's OK… I'll find a YES." Someone lets you down? "That's OK… I'll find someone who won't." Your job won't promote you? "That's OK… I'll find one that will."

No self-blame. Just high standards. That's how you find peace in life because your standards remind you that you'll always make the right decision because you know what you deserve and your past taught you WHY you deserve it.

Picky or selective?

Part 2. ROI, Baby

When you have high standards, I hope you celebrate the ROI you'll eventually get from hanging onto them. Don't become full of yourself or entitled in any sense, but recognize that when you have high standards AND you live them consistently, you *should* expect good things and good people to come into your life. Your high standards won't allow anything less, and it's good to have a mentality that expects high ROI.

Do you expect great things to happen in your life?

I do. I expect great things to happen to me but not because I deserve them for simply being alive or because I think I'm the greatest. I expect them to happen because I'm willing to suffer for those things. I'm willing to work for them tirelessly and stubbornly.

If you played competitive sports growing up, I'm sure you heard your coach at some point give you the tried-and-true line of, "This is why we practice," "No pain no gain," or, "Suffer now so we perform tomorrow." You worked your a** off in practice or you pushed yourself to exhaustion because you wanted what was on the other side of the exertion.

I'm sure you've heard this question before, but now seems like a good time to bring it up in the context of standards: "What are you willing to suffer for in life?"

This is such a classic and powerful question because now when you're "suffering" - you're frustrated, you're getting your a** kicked, rejected, disappointed, etc. - you can fall back on knowing it's worth it because YOU decided it's worth it.

WHAT is worth suffering for? WHO is worth suffering for? What process are you willing to endure?

That's the ultimate question, and answering it is a one-way ticket to being more hopeful about what comes next in your life. If you stand for something, if you want it badly, and it guides you completely... you're willing to suffer for it and that means something!

It means something to say, "I want this, I deserve this... AND I'm willing to suffer for it!" Because then when you're going through tough times, you can remember WHY. And having a WHY is what makes you hopeful. WHY makes you stubborn, and stubbornness makes you hopeful.

Why do you go on bad date after bad date? Why do you get rejected? Why do you get up again after being ghosted? Why do you put in hours at work? Why do you take time to work on your passion projects even though you're just getting started? You do those things because you're willing to suffer through the process of finding someone special, accomplishing your goals, or finding fulfillment in your creative life. You recognize the ROI that suffering offers you.

Why do you feel bogged down at work? Why do you feel unappreciated at your job? Uninspired, plateaued? Why do you feel insecure? Why do you feel a lack of confidence, direction, or passion in life? Why do you feel forgotten or left behind sometimes? It's not because you deserve to feel those things. It's because those feelings are part of the process of becoming secure, confident, and fulfilled. Suffering through that process is part of what happens when you decide to stand for building yourself into the best person you can be.

It's not about always finding a silver lining in life. I simply see the process quite logically. In life, there are "wanters" and "doers." There are people who say, "I want great things," and they think they'll just attract those things and that they're doing their part by manifesting with their morning coffee.

And then there are people who say, "I want great things," and they go out and prove it by how much of the process they're willing to suffer through to make it a reality.

Having something you're willing to suffer for is what separates you in life. It sucks to feel frustrated, overlooked, lost, forgotten, or like a failure... But can you find hope in knowing that you made a choice for what you stand for?... and that means something.

Whatever your "thing is," you have decided you're willing to suffer for it in order to be proud of yourself. That means if you have to have an awkward conversation with someone, you'll suffer through it. If that means you shoot your shot and get rejected again and again, you'll suffer through it. You stand for being proud of yourself, knowing that you went after what you want and you know it's gonna suck... but you're willing to suffer for it. Can you say that?

"I'm willing to be frustrated, rejected, have a bad day, a bad week, a bad month. I'm willing to feel that weight on my shoulders, the pressure, the temptation to feel lost. I'm willing to!"

I don't know about you, but suffering through inevitable ups and downs in life makes me hopeful. Because I know that good things come to those who are willing to suffer. Can you wipe the slate clean right now and forgive yourself for giving up in the past? For not standing up tall when things didn't go your way?

Feeling negative emotions is part of the process.

**Forgive yourself for all the times
you didn't think you were good enough,
smart enough, or worthy enough.**

I wish the path to the great and rewarding things in life were simple and not draining.

But that's not the reality we face. Great art comes from suffering. Great novels from torment. Dating the wrong person eventually leads to the right person. Getting fired from your job frees you up to find and evolve to the right one. Practicing and putting in hours and hours and hours of work makes you a great athlete. Putting in the hours at your corporate job is what gets you promoted. Heck, this very book came from my own experience "suffering" through living my own version of gray to come to these realizations.

We know there is a reward at the end of hard work, of ups and downs. We don't always know when or how, but that is why we choose to do the things we do. And within the context of choosing one or two or three BIG things in life that are so important to you that you're willing to suffer for them… you can choose to have this same belief. That's a belief that good things are coming your way. That's a commitment to a vision, a commitment to a standard, a commitment to what you want and deserve… and means that you'll eventually get it. You just have to put up with the BS in the meantime.

People who are the happiest couples, the most fulfilled corporate leaders, the happiest and most creative artists and musicians… Each one went through this suffering process. They know what and who was worth suffering for in their lives because they experienced the opposite.

The person who found their perfect partner was once in a toxic relationship. The most fulfilled corporate leader was once working the mail room and hating their job. The happiest artist or musician was told on multiple occasions that their art or music was trash. They suffered through those experiences because they decided at some point that they stood for something and they recognized the process would try to derail them.

But they were bold and persisted because they had asked themselves this question:

"What is worth suffering for? Who is worth suffering for?"

The rewarding thing about life is that not only does answering that question make you a centered, powerful, and resilient person… but that belief is what brings you together with other people who have the same mentality. You're willing to suffer for someone who believes the same and stands for it? I believe the universe will conspire to bring you two together. You're gonna have to weed through a lot of negativity and wrong people, but that belief brings people together.

Those "suffering" moments of the process remind you that it will pay off, and eventually, you'll look back and realize just how far you've come… just by standing for something. Just by being willing to suffer! You can call it the law of attraction or manifesting. I simply call it "hopeful stubbornness."

Part 3. What Are the Odds?

Here comes the fine print: suffering for something comes with a large family-sized, all you can eat buffet serving of NO. It comes with a lot of disappointment and rejection.

My usual headline for handling rejection is, "Knowing is better than not knowing." I will always say that it's better to hear NO than to never hear anything at all. I stand by that! No regrets in life. That's all well and good until you find yourself shooting your shot, putting yourself out there, asking for what you want and deserve but you keep hearing NO, NO, NO, no thanks, or not right now over and over again. The idea of, "It's better to have a story to tell than no story at all" loses its charm after being rejected repeatedly and you end up thinking, "OK, yes it's better to know than to not know, but now I'm tempted to know that I suck and I'm meant for a life of NO."

So, here's how I've come to evolve my thinking about rejection. I've seen startup founders really lean into this idea, and originally I used this idea in my sales career - because there's no experience more ripe with hearing NO than sales.

The idea is you have to learn to celebrate hearing NO. And, how do you do that? You prove to yourself that each NO is actually moving you closer to YES. Each NO is statistically moving you closer to YES.

The method I've borrowed goes like this:

First, sit down and figure out what your goal is. That's the YES you want to hear. That's the thing you're willing to suffer for. It could be the YES to getting your dream job. It could be the YES to getting signed to that record label. It could be the YES to finding your dream person. It's the YES to whatever it is that you've determined is "success" in your life.

Second, sit down, and this isn't exact science and you shouldn't overthink it, BUT try to calculate the odds of succeeding or the odds of hearing that YES - as in for one YES you're going to need to hear 50 NOs.

Calculate the odds. There's obviously no way to know how many NOs you're going to need to hear, but just sit down and pick something honestly and intuitively. In my sales career, for example, I knew that in order to close one deal, it took an average of five meetings with a prospective client to make it happen. So, I knew the more meetings I took and the more NOs I heard, the closer I was to closing a deal.

In your dating life, for instance, you could say it might take you 20 crappy dates to finally find someone you deserve. OK, that's your number. In your career, you could say it might take you three jobs until you get your dream job. OK, that's your number. In your creative endeavor, you could say it might take hearing NO 20 times before you hear YES and you get that book deal, movie deal, etc. OK, that's your number.

Calculate the odds of the YES you want to hear. Just come up with a number that reflects the value of what you want. If it's really important to you, you're probably going to need to hear more NOs, so reflect that in the number you pick.

Maybe when you thought you were rejected from what you wanted... you were just being redirected to what you needed.

Now rejection is simply a numbers game. For every NO you hear at work, for every frustrating bad date you go on, and for every curveball thrown your way... you are statistically improving your odds of getting to YES. I'm pretty sure that's how statistical probability works - if you need to hear five NOs before a YES, each NO moves you 20% closer to the result you want (assuming your efforts are connected and you're never "starting from zero").

Life, of course, isn't that simple, and will never align with probability, but we can logically approach hearing NO. It's never going to take away the sting from being rejected, but it will help you to quickly flip a switch to realize that each rejection is proof that you're getting closer. Your odds are literally improving each time you hear NO. I know this might sound rather robotic, but I think it's a compassionate lens to look at life through.

It's tough to put a number on how many partners you need before you find "the one" or how many bad dates you need to go on, but the key to keep going in life is to incentivize yourself to try again. In the case of the least robotic area of life - dating - you can turn to this logic each time you hear, "Sorry we're not a good fit," for every person who doesn't see your worth, or who doesn't choose you or you don't choose them and know you're statistically improving your odds of finding someone who does.

Each time YOU'RE willing to put yourself in the game, each time you're willing to try first, to love first, to be hurt and learn from it, each time you're willing to live your standard and shoot your shot…. you're statistically improving your odds of getting what you want and deserve.

The people and experiences you want in life are not just going to show up at your door. They will come from trial and error. They will come from YOUR willingness to try. They will come from your willingness to say YES, from going on dates, meeting other people, making calls, starting over… and getting as close to that number as you need.

Each NO you hear means you're getting closer to the last time you'll hear NO. There's no science to this, but the quality of your life - how happy you are as you go after what you want - comes down to your mindset and how quickly you can recover from disappointment and how gracefully you're able to roll with the punches. What are the odds?

CHAPTER SIXTEEN

Imposter, Who?

****

Life is short. Dive headfirst into what excites you. Go on that trip. Love the people who matter to you most. Eat the last slice.

Choose kindness over gossip. Choose forgiveness over grudges. Do what scares you. Be grateful for all the blessings you have in your life and create even more.

Part 1. Feelin' Cute, Won't Delete Later

You deserve to feel the same love, respect, attention, and support you give others. If you're willing to do the things you want to receive, then without a doubt, no overthinking and no imposter syndrome... you deserve to receive the same in return.

That's how you rationalize what you deserve. That's how you prove what you deserve. It's simple, and the answer is always yes. If you're willing to do it yourself, you deserve it. It might not be on the exact timeline you want, it might not be all at once, it might not be in the form you expect... but you deserve those things. Your worth doesn't change based on someone or something's inability to reciprocate what you offer.

Sounds simple, right? But then imposter syndrome rears its ugly head and you're quick to talk yourself out of what you deserve. You're quick to throw your standards out the window, lower the bar, and settle.

Imposter syndrome: You don't belong. You're faking it. You don't deserve success, good things, or happiness. You're going to be discovered sooner or later. You can put any label you want on it, but the idea of imposter syndrome is an ever-present, sinking feeling of self-doubt. You say you deserve good things in life - success, happiness, connection, fulfillment, to be respected and loved - but then there's this lingering doubt that says, "But do you really?"

For example, when someone praises you or says you're great or amazing or whatever compliment they're dishing up, you think they're just patronizing you. In your head you say, "Pshhhh if only they knew. They're just saying that. They don't mean it."

Or if you accomplish a goal, make a new friend, a date went well, or you found your groove... you think to yourself,

"This is just a momentary lapse and I'll be reverted to what I actually deserve soon. It was fun while it lasted."

It's very easy to negatively reframe your worth in life. It's easy to find a way to justify thinking you don't actually deserve the things you deserve. We're all quick to lower our opinion of ourselves even when life around us shows the opposite. To snap out of imposter syndrome, I recommend focusing on one word: reciprocity.

Follow the logic of reciprocity. If you're willing to love someone, you deserve to be loved. If you're willing to support someone, you deserve to be supported. If you're willing to respect someone, you deserve to be respected. If you're willing to be honest with someone, you deserve to receive the same honesty. If you're willing to give someone time, attention, and compassion...you deserve to also receive someone's time, attention, and compassion.

What you deserve is built 100% on reciprocity, and when you return to that place of power and logic, I hope you'll find the strength to ignore your nagging imposter syndrome.

If you've ever wondered what hot, smart, and worthy look like in one person, just look in the mirror.

As long as you're willing to do the things you say you want - and you do them - I don't see how it's possible that you don't deserve them. Logically. 1+1 always equals 2. That's the beauty of self-worth! You can prove your worth.

It's not enough in life to just say you deserve something simply because you're alive. No.

You deserve something because you're willing to give the very things you want to receive. You deserve something because of what you're willing to DO in order to receive it.

You don't deserve love, success, or fulfillment simply because you're alive. Sorry. Of course, you deserve basic things like respect, common decency, access to equal opportunity, and fair treatment, but beyond that, the things you want and deserve are built entirely on what YOU do. That's the beauty of PROVING your self-worth and never forgetting it.

The moment you're willing to love someone else, the moment you're vulnerable enough to do the things you want to receive, the moment you're willing to be hurt, the moment you're willing to show someone you love them with your words, actions, or support, you become worthy of those things yourself. You become worthy of experiencing the same things you're willing to give and do.

Your worth is all about you. It's always been about you. It will always be about you. If you're willing to do something, you deserve the same in return. At minimum, you deserve the opportunity to receive the same in return. But sometimes it isn't returned to you. How many times have you been hurt? How many times have you given but not received? How many times have you been compassionate, supportive, and loved someone but didn't receive the same? Probably quite a few times.

> **Someone's inability to give you what you deserve doesn't change what you deserve.**

But that doesn't mean you didn't deserve that thing. It doesn't mean you still don't deserve it. In those instances, it simply meant that person or circumstance didn't recognize that. It doesn't change your worth. It just changed the timing, the person, or the context. You deserve all the things you say you deserve. You deserve them for the simple reason that you're willing to do them yourself.

And it's sometimes helpful also to flip the script to other people.

When you're getting to know someone, consider this question in relation to their behavior. Do they deserve the things they say they want? They say they want honesty and compassion and commitment. Well, are they willing to give it?

Judge yourself through this lens and judge others in the same way. If you're not willing to do the things you say you deserve, I'm not surprised you doubt yourself. But it's an easy fix! It's all about what you're willing to do, what you're willing to practice, and what you're willing to give. It's all about the empathy you're willing to offer, the support, the respect, the honesty, and the compassion you give others.

The moment you're willing to give those things to others, that's the moment you deserve them in return.

"I am worthy today and I am worthy tomorrow because I am willing to do the things I say I deserve."

In the heat of the moment, remind yourself of your worth and stand your ground. "Am I actively practicing this thing?" Yes? Then remain grounded in your worth. You deserve to be supported, respected, and treated with honest love and kindness. That's how you know.

No overthinking. Reciprocity. No imposter syndrome. You deserve to feel the same love, respect, attention, and support you give others.

Part 2. Unqualified Is a State of Mind

In the face of feeling unworthy, not ready, or unqualified… remember one word: DESPITE. In the face of feeling unqualified to get a spot, unqualified to date someone, to work somewhere, or to get the spotlight, remember one word: DESPITE.

Sometimes to combat imposter syndrome, I find a form of visualization helpful. I call it the power of "UN." That's the power of feeling untalented. Unexpected. Unqualified. Unusual. Unlikely. Unworthy. Unassuming. Unfit. Unknown. Unbold.

I picture a headline that describes me that way:

"He was an unlikely candidate for the job, but despite that…"

"He was the most unexpected success of the year, but despite that…"

"He was unqualified, but despite that…"

A headline like that speaks to my imposter syndrome, but then I turn to the power of DESPITE. You can do all kinds of things DESPITE what you think is the reason you can't. I like to think of it as a challenge. Unqualified? Unexpected? Unlikely? Unusual? Yet… here you are, DESPITE that assumption, still moving forward. DESPITE that feeling, here you are doing that thing.

Show yourself that the path to doing what you want is not a straight shot where you ditch all feelings of imposter syndrome or doubt.

It's riddled with self-doubt and imposter syndrome, but you continue along that path one step after another DESPITE that feeling.

You shoot your shot DESPITE how unlikely you think it is you'll hear YES. You create that passion project DESPITE how unexpected it is coming from you. You ask for that promotion DESPITE how unqualified you think you'll come off as.

Take it as a challenge. Picture the headline. The largest, most memorable headlines in life are the ones that usually describe a DESPITE moment, right? The world loves a good underdog story.

… winning the world series DESPITE being 45 years old.

… getting cast in that movie DESPITE never having landed a major role before.

… getting that dream job offer DESPITE thinking everyone else was better qualified.

… creating a hit single DESPITE never having a hit before.

Those are the headlines people read and remember. Why can't that be you? Well, it can be… if you embrace the power of DESPITE.

You look happier since you decided you're worthy of more despite what your anxiety tells you.

Embrace the "UNs" your humanness dishes up to you on a silver platter. See them as a challenge.

Despite your imposter syndrome, you are doing your thing and you're going for it. Show yourself that those feelings are real, but they are irrelevant. "UN" is irrelevant. Feeling unlikely, unexpected, unqualified, or untalented is irrelevant.

All you're looking at is WHAT you do. The things you do. The commitment you have to do them. Again and again and again. The things you ask for. The shots you take. The hours you put in.

That's where your focus lies, and you see the path forward because of that focus. The path is not a straight one, but it's a path you're committed to DESPITE what you sometimes feel.

You succeed, you overcome, and you grow DESPITE the labels you put on yourself. You succeed, you overcome, and you grow DESPITE the NOs you hear along the way. You succeed, you overcome, and you grow DESPITE the misunderstanding someone might have of you.

Try saying this:

"At this point in my life, I feel what I feel - scared, nervous, insecure, anxious - but I do it anyway."

Embrace the "UNs" in your life. See them as a challenge. You have to find a way to keep going. You need something lighting a fire under you or otherwise when you hear that fifth NO, you're going to hang up your cleats and call it a day - and I wouldn't blame you. Without a fire, it's tough to keep going.

Acknowledge the feelings, don't ignore them. Heck, they might even be true. You might be unexpected. You might be unqualified. But you're doing it DESPITE that. You're doing it DESPITE the feelings. That's what keeps you going. Empowered stubbornness. Vision.

Life rewards people on their 10th try. Life rewards people on their 100th podcast episode, their 26th job application, their 30th audition, their 10th book, their 100th YouTube video.

Embrace the power of DESPITE. See the "UN." Look it in the eye and decide it's not in your way. You're going through it DESPITE that feeling. Unlikely, unexpected, unqualified, or untalented? That's irrelevant.

Part 3. Facts vs. Feelings

When it comes to the "UNs" and the negative emotions we feel in our lives, we need to learn to adopt a mindset of seeing them but not giving them any room to grow. I'm sure you've heard the advice, "Honor your feelings but don't trust them." I think this is great advice because I've realized WHY it's practically necessary. Here's how I look at our emotions and what it means to "be in touch" with how you feel.

Being in touch with your emotions is attractive.

Think about how we've trained ourselves to have our guards up when it comes to other people - we don't take everything other people say at face value; we look for proof that something is true, and we get to know them BEFORE we arrive at a conclusion. We honor their presence with respect, but it takes time before we fully trust them. That's how it should be! Some people are all talk. Some people aren't what they seem. It's a good thing to need to see proof before you trust someone fully.

Why don't we treat our own emotions the same way? Why don't we honor our feelings, but not trust them right away?

That is how we differentiate between facts and feelings. Feel what you feel. But don't trust that feeling immediately. Observe it first.

There have been various studies in which scientists have approached topics regarding where thoughts originate; are they even ours? In one study, two scientists, David Oakley from University College London and Peter Halligan from Cardiff University, suggested we have no control over our thoughts in the first place.

Their theory, published in Frontiers in Psychology, says, "The contents of consciousness are generated 'behind the scenes' by fast, efficient, non-conscious systems in our brains.

All this happens without any interference from our personal awareness, which sits passively in the passenger seat while these processes occur." Put simply, we don't consciously choose our thoughts or our feelings – we become aware of them." [1]

So, there is a difference between our thoughts and self-aware thoughts? They might not be one and the same? If that's the case, maybe we can stop rationalizing our thoughts as a subtle conclusion that we really believe about ourselves?

In the study, Oakley and Halligan used biologist Thomas Henry Huxley's metaphor of a train to describe the relationship between the mind and the brain. They say the relationship is similar to a steam whistle and an engine. The steam whistle acts in response to the work of the engine, but has no influence over it. Similarly, consciousness is the product of the brain. It cannot control it. [2]

Scientist and SF State Associate Professor of Psychology, Ezequiel Morsella, also examined how thoughts that lead to actions enter our consciousness. He ultimately showed that many of our thoughts are simply involuntary. While we can "decide" to think about certain things, other information - including activities we have learned like counting - can enter our subconscious and cause us to think about something else, whether we want to or not. [3]

In the first experiment, 35 students were told beforehand to not count an array of objects presented to them. In 90% of the trials, students counted the objects involuntarily. In a second experiment, students were presented with differently colored geometric shapes and given the option of either naming the colors or counting the shapes. Even though students chose one over the other, around 40 percent thought about both sets.

"The data support the view that when one is performing a desired action, conscious thoughts about alternative plans still occupy the mind, often insuppressibly," said Morsella. [4] The study's findings support Morsella's passive frame theory, which suggests that most thoughts enter our brains as a result of subliminal processes we don't totally control.

Don't let that freak you out. It's good news. If we aren't in complete control of the thoughts that enter our minds and they're often separate from our own awareness and what we know to be true, it means we have the ability to exert our realities on those thoughts. We have the ability to hit pause and question the emotions we feel BEFORE we buy into them completely.

We can approach our emotions in the same way we approach our relationships with other people. We tend to approach other people with a bit of healthy doubt. It's not super cynical or untrusting, but it's just a sense of, "I don't know this person so lemme see what's up before I'm bought into them. Lemme feel them out, lemme ask them some questions before I start to trust them."

That's smart! Feel them out, see if they're legit, real, and authentic, and then you can move to trust them and invite them into your life. But before that, you're going to be respectful, nice, and open, but you're not going to have a 100% level of trust just yet.

Why don't we learn to approach our feelings in the same way? Why don't we learn to honor them, respect them, not ignore them... but question them BEFORE we start to trust them?

Live, laugh, listen to your intuition.

In the same way that some people don't belong in our lives - they don't deserve your trust or our energy - many of our feelings are the same. And we really only realize that if we take time to pause and question them.

Is this feeling a reflection of what I actually believe? Is this true? Or is this a temporary feeling brought about by circumstances that are temporary? Is how I'm feeling a fact? Is this feeling something I strongly believe or is it a feeling - a temporary reaction to the temporary circumstances of life?

A fact. That's something you strongly believe in and have proven: I am worthy. I am capable. I am lovable. My hard work will pay off. A feeling. That's something that is situational based on circumstances: I am invisible. I'm lost. I'm falling behind. No one appreciates me.

Facts vs. feelings.

Honor the feeling but pause before you trust it. Open the front door, and before you invite that feeling in and before you ask it to take its shoes off and stay a while, question it: "Who are you? Are you real? Is this the real me? Or is this a temporary feeling that does not define me and doesn't belong in my house?"

Give yourself the gift of pausing for a moment: "Is this a feeling I should trust right away? Should I trust this feeling at face value?"

"I'm feeling lost, unlovable, unworthy." "WHY should I trust this feeling as a fact right now? What evidence do I have that this is real and permanent? What proof do I have that this is a feeling I should trust?"

Hopefully when you address a feeling like this, you'll realize it's temporary and not a description of WHO you are but rather of how you FEEL. This is NOT easy, of course, but the more you train yourself to question the emotions you feel, the more you'll start to see that the feeling doesn't have a strong case for belonging in your life.

In a court of law, it's not a strong case. It's circumstantial evidence at best, your honor. The feeling is the feeling because you've been feeling it. That's it.

Yes, it's the result of life and events and randomness, but if you zoom out, I'm hoping you'll see that it's very much tied to circumstance. And because circumstance can change, you'll realize that you can honor the feeling but decide to NOT trust it. You can honor the feeling as just that - a feeling - but you don't allow it to become a fact.

THAT is the gift of being human. YOU get to decide what are the facts in your life. You get to decide if you ARE unworthy, unlovable, lost, or untalented or if you just FEEL that way. You get to decide if the feelings are allowed into your house. You get to decide if they are worthy of a seat at your table.

It's tough for all of us to talk about emotions. Maybe that's the problem? We don't know how to handle feelings, and rather than dig in and get serious about analyzing them, we just accept them as fact. But we are so incredibly capable of honoring our feelings but not trusting them.

The next time you get an incoming feeling where you feel anxious, insecure, doubtful, or unworthy… say, "I'm going to pause. Before I say this is who I am, before I make a conclusion about my potential based on this feeling… I'm going to question it." When you do, you'll realize that you can feel anxious, but it doesn't mean you're falling behind. You can feel unworthy, but that's just because someone - one person or two people - didn't see what you bring to the table. And that's their loss. You can feel like you're lost, but it doesn't mean you can't find your stride… like tomorrow.

Compare those feelings to the facts you know to be true.

This book has been all about the facts in your life. What are the facts you believe in?

What are the big, zoomed out truths in your life that you refuse to negotiate on? What are the facts you can turn to to PROVE that a feeling is just a feeling and doesn't need to be trusted?

"I am worthy of honesty because I am honest and bold."

"My hard work will pay off because I'm willing to put in the work."

"I am worthy of the same energy and effort put into a relationship."

FACTS. Those are FACTS that you refuse to negotiate on. Those are FACTS that you can turn to in the moments where you hit pause. Those are FACTS you can turn to in the moments where you honor a feeling, but you don't trust it.

Is this a fact or a feeling?

CHAPTER SEVENTEEN

Reintroduce Yourself

****

You can be

beautiful AND talented…
quiet AND confident…
in love AND independent…
grateful AND ambitious…
eccentric AND professional…
strong AND sensitive…

at the same time.

Part 1. Take Your Own Advice

What advice would you give your younger self? Don't overthink it. Just give the simplest, most obvious, first thing that pops into your head.

For me I would say, "Younger Case, enjoy life WHILE you're living it."

That's an easy answer for me. That's the advice I would confidently give my younger self, but it's in direct contrast to how I tend to live my life. Admittedly, I'm not great at calming down and appreciating what I have currently, what I'm doing currently, or who I am at the moment. I'm always moving the finish line with, "I just need to do this, and grow this, and work on this… and then I'll be satisfied."

I'm sure you can relate to your own personal hypocrisy, and it begs the question: "Why don't we take our own advice in life?" I don't have a great answer to that. I'm sure it has something to do with all the things we've reviewed so far - pressure to conform, conditioning, comfort, comparison, etc. Personally, I'm great at rationalizing NOT taking my own advice by saying things like, "It's because I'm a driven person. I'm just really ambitious, but eventually I'll settle down."

How do I reconcile this with the fact that I'd so confidently tell my younger self to do the opposite of what I'm currently doing? Why don't we take our own advice? Why do we ignore our intuitions?

Maybe you're the friend who gives great advice. I'm talking top tier *chef's kiss* advice. You give your friends helpful advice and perspective when it comes to their dating lives or their career. When it's not your life, you can see things clearly and you give genuinely helpful advice, BUT when it comes to your own life, you don't take it - not even close.

Or maybe you're fully aware of what the right advice is in your life, but you rarely actually act on it. You're aware of some of your self-destructive tendencies, but you don't take your own advice to stop them. "I should really eat healthier. I should really stop hooking up with randos. I should really get disciplined about work. I should really go after that thing I'm passionate about. I should really stop watering myself down to fit in."

But then when it's game time, you're at *Trader Joe's* getting groceries, you're swiping on the dating apps, you're out at the bar, or you're mindlessly scrolling on Instagram... you suddenly lose sight of that advice. You resort to what you normally do. You resort to comfort. You resort to stubbornness. You resort to fitting in.

Stop leaning on some of the common excuses we all turn to.

"I'm getting older and it's too late to take that advice."

"I'm not getting any younger. I can't start over; I can't slow down."

We use age a lot as an excuse. We use experience as an excuse as well - "I can't change now. I've invested too much into this habit, this endeavor, this mindset, or this timeline."

To take our own advice for once in life, we need to think smaller. We can throw those common age-related excuses out by committing to doing something small and different for just one day. That's it. Change comes from one day of taking your own advice.

You're better off changing your mind than hoping something will eventually change.

State your advice, and then instead of kicking it down the road like you always do and instead of dishing it out to your friends but not doing it yourself... take your own advice for one day and see what happens.

We are all capable of actually taking our own advice, but to convince our silly and stubborn human selves to do it, we need to think small, not big.

We don't need to think, "I'm going to be healthier FOREVER. I'm going to eat and work out every day FOREVER. I'm going to quit my job and start my own business for the rest of my life. I'm going to be confident FOREVER. I'm going to be FOREVER grateful each day."

We need to think smaller:

"TODAY I'm going to eat healthy. TODAY I'm going to work out. TODAY I'm going to write down my business idea. TODAY I'm going to slow down."

"TODAY I'm going to take my own advice. And then I'm going to do it again tomorrow." That is how we end up taking our own advice in the long run. We think small, and small moments show us that it's never too late to do something new, different, or simpler.

What advice would you give your younger self? Don't overthink it. What's the first piece of advice you'd give yourself? Are you taking your own advice? I'd venture to say you're not or you're not fully. Otherwise, why would you tell your young self that? It's likely a change from your current habits or something you wish you started doing sooner. So, there's likely something holding you back from taking your own advice.

You can certainly take some time and dive into what that might be and why that's the case... but ultimately, can you push yourself to take one step and take your advice TODAY?

Just take your own advice today. That's just one day of taking your advice. And then do it again tomorrow. You don't need to commit to a forever version of that advice because I think that is what holds us back from taking it in the first place - thinking too big and making too much of a commitment.

That's when we allow our human excuses to kick in - "I don't have time for that, that's too much of a change, I'm running out of time," etc.

What advice would you give your younger self?

"Slow down. Appreciate what you have. Don't take life for granted."

"Stop waiting for the perfect moment to act. Don't compare yourself. Be yourself. Be kind to yourself."

Great advice! What's stopping you from living that today? There's a reason you know that advice to be true. The experiences in your life have shown you why it's true and why it's important. Why would you tell your younger self to embrace it otherwise? Don't ignore it anymore. Take your own advice. Do it on a small scale. Do it today. Don't freak yourself out. Don't let your human self resort to robot mode or excuse mode - "I'm too old, I'm past that point, I don't have time, I can't stop now." Don't allow yourself to go to that place because your vision is too big.

Think small. Smaller, smaller, smaller, a bit smaller. Yes, right there.

Self-love is taking your own advice and finally deciding you deserve better.

"Today I'm going to slow down and appreciate what I have. Today is the perfect moment to take one step towards that thing I've always put off. Today I'm not going to compare myself at all. Today I'm going to be 100% true to myself. Today I'm going to compliment myself and be kind to ME."

Do it today. And then when you wake up tomorrow, take your own advice again. And eventually you'll be proud of yourself because you're finally taking your own advice in big ways, but for now, you start small. What advice would you give your younger self?

Part 2. Take a Step Back

What should you do when you don't know what to do at all? What should you do when you don't have any advice to give? You're at a loss. You're stuck. You're confused. What should you do when you don't know if your standard is being met in dating? What should you do if you're confused about whether your boss is really a jerk or you're just being sensitive? What should you do if you feel completely lost or unfulfilled in life?

What should you do in those instances where, by your own admission, you simply don't know what to do? "What should I do?"

Try some role-play. Instead of getting lost in overthinking or giving up, pretend your friend asked you that same question. Pretend it was their life in the context of the question and they simply asked you... "Hey, what should I do?"

If a friend asked you that, what would you say? If you're dating someone and they keep giving you mixed signals, they're acting sketchy, or they're hot and cold and you're unsure of what to do because you want it to work so badly. What should you do? Pretend a friend asked you that question. "I'm dating someone and they keep giving me mixed signals, they're acting sketchy, and they're hot and cold... I'm unsure of what to do. What should I do?"

Well, what's your gut reaction to that? You'd probably say, "You deserve better. You deserve someone who's sure and isn't playing games."

You're stressed out at work, you're overworked, your boss is entirely too demanding, micromanaging you, and they don't respect your personal life. You're torn because you want to be promoted and you want to succeed. What should you do? If a friend asked you that, what would you say? "I'm stressed out at work, I'm overworked, my boss is entirely too demanding, is a micromanager, and doesn't respect my personal life... What should I do?" Well, what's your gut reaction to that? You'd probably say, "You deserve better balance. You need to speak up or move on."

Why do we sometimes struggle to see the objective, obvious answers in life?

A while back, I saw a post on Reddit titled, "What is the most helpful thing your therapist has ever said to you?" The top comment was as follows and it gave me a lightbulb moment when it comes to this idea of not knowing what to do:

"My therapist and I were discussing how I felt about a pretty deep betrayal from my now ex-wife. I was beating myself up for not seeing how bad she really was when there was plenty of evidence. My therapist wrote down something on his yellow notepad and then held it up right in my face, practically touching my nose.

He said, 'What's that say?'

I couldn't read it; it was too close to my face. Stepping back from it a bit, I could read that it said, 'You're too close to see it.' He was right.

I was too close to the problems and the situation to have been able to see it where in retrospect, it was so obvious. I stopped beating myself up over it and was able to let it go." [1]

YES! That's it! We are hyper aware of every detail of everything in our lives, we're consumed by them, we overthink them, we're unable to detach from them, and we live them 24/7. Sometimes we're just so close to the issues we face in life to see the obvious answer.

That's the obvious answer we'd see if we found a way to step back for just a moment.

Your story is so much more than the limits of its previous chapters.

If a friend asked you that, what would you say?

What would you say when you try just for a moment to be a bit more objective? To be a teeny tiny bit less involved or less consumed by that thing? Maybe you'd give yourself some tough love that says... "OK, this is ridiculous, I see it now. I've been hanging onto this for too long, I've been putting up with this, I've been blind to the obvious truth... because I'm so close to this thing."

That is the paradox of life. To discover what's best for you, you have to be close to yourself. You have to be close to the question at hand, to the feelings you have that inform you of your essence, and your intuition. You have to get your hands dirty, you have to be vulnerable, and go through it. You need that deep and vulnerable introspection to discover what's best for you in life. But you also need to find a way to look at those things objectively. You need to find a way to observe and not feel.

You need to find a way to do the inner-work and be honest with yourself, but then take a step back and check yourself. This is how you embrace your ability to be bold.

So, in the instances where you simply don't know what to do, check that you're not so close to the thing, to the question, to the insecurity, to the frustration that you're unable to observe with objectivity. Are you so close that you can't see what's obvious? Sometimes the most powerful thing in life is your ability to just observe without feeling.

If a friend asked you that, what would you say?

Part 3. You're the Kind of Person Who...

I love defining myself with verbs.

Part Two and Three of this book have been about actions - things you can DO and SAY to get yourself out of the gray in life. Verbs mean action, and I'm all about action. I'm all about being curious and figuring things out in life - not sitting around and hoping I figure them out, but instead doing, acting, asking, traveling, etc. I'm all about VERBing to figure life out.

We get ourselves in a lot of trouble because we put way too much pressure on ourselves with the way we describe ourselves. That's the way we describe who we want to be or how we describe our ideal selves. The words we use in life are important, and as small a thing as it might seem, it's very important to describe yourself with verbs instead of adjectives.

"I want to be confident. I want to be happy. I want to be successful."

There's a lot of pressure inherent in phrases like that because when you invariably fall short of those adjectives, you feel like crap. You feel like a fake. You feel like an imposter.

"I'm supposed to be confident, but I'm not right now, so that means I'm a loser. I'm supposed to be happy, but I'm not right now, so that means I'm destined to live a sad life. I'm supposed to be successful, but I'm not right now, so that means I'm a failure."

Let's switch from adjectives to verbs and see what happens. Personally, I like defining myself by what I do because that's a goal I can get behind 24/7 and it's something that can never be taken from me.

What verbs actually define you? What do you DO?

A goal like, "I want to be happy" is tough because you're not always going to be happy. Happiness is a state of mind. Objectively, happiness can be taken from you by other people, bad luck, or randomness. But life and randomness can't take the VERBS you do from you. Instead of saying, "I want to be happy," I say, "I'm the kind of person who's willing to try new things, who practices gratitude, and who respects himself." No one can take those VERBS from me, and I'm convinced those verbs will ultimately make me happy.

We all owe it to ourselves to stop putting so much pressure on ourselves to BE a certain way - to describe ourselves with cut and dry words, adjectives, and visions - and instead, we should use words to describe the things we do that will make us that way.

Your confidence to be weird and different is undeniably attractive.

The words we use matter, and if we're not intentional with them, we put too much pressure on ourselves. When we have pressure on ourselves, we act strangely. We do weird things. We lower our standards and we get in our heads.

When we try to define ourselves by saying, "I am successful, I am happy, I am attractive, I am funny, I am driven, or I am motivated." Or "I want to be successful, happy, or attractive," we get ourselves in trouble. I, of course, think it's great to be those things and strive to be those things myself, but when we define ourselves in that way and when we inevitably fall short - when we have a bad day at work, we drop the ball, we feel lazy, we overeat or overdrink - we get in our heads about it. We beat ourselves up. We think we're falling behind compared to other people. We start saying we're unworthy, lazy, or talentless, etc.

Try defining yourself with verbs rather than adjectives. I certainly define myself as someone who is successful or at least aspires to be successful. Of course I want to be happy. Of course I want to always be driven. But I think it's better to reframe that to say, "You're the kind of person who...."

Instead of saying, "I want to be confident," I say, "I'm the kind of person who is willing to try, asks for what he wants, and tries new things." Those VERBS build confidence, and those are things I can control. I can't always control whether I feel confident because of course there are days I won't. On those days, I'll really beat myself up, but I can control what I do and the words I use to describe myself - the verbs I use to describe myself.

Instead of saying, "I want to be happy," I say, "I'm the kind of person who is grateful for the life I'm building." That is something I can practice every day. I can wake up each morning and be grateful for the privilege of being able to write for a living, to drink coffee in the morning, and to have people who love and support me.

The way you describe yourself and the goals you set for yourself are both areas in life that are ripe with frustration. When I think about my own life and where I've tripped up mentally before - where I think I missed my shot, where I'm falling short, where I feel that I'm missing out - it was because of the way I perceived myself. I assigned too much permanence to the adjectives I had attached to myself and my goals for myself.

As we've reviewed, it's human nature to assume everyone else has their life figured out and you don't. We think everyone else has a grand plan for their career, for their happiness, and for their dating life.

The best counter to stop beating yourself up for when you feel lost, less, or not focused is to sit down and do this exercise.

Think of the things you want to accomplish and who you aspire to be and describe yourself with VERBS. Turn those adjectives into verbs. Action. Doing. VERBing.

You want to be happy? Well, what are the verbs? You're the kind of person who practices gratitude every day, who eats healthy, who washes their face, who stays hydrated?

You want to be successful? Well, what are the verbs? You're the kind of person who does what they say they'll do, you're the kind of person who submits work on time, you're the kind of person who asks for a promotion, you're the kind of person who volunteers to go first?

You want to be in a healthy relationship? Well, what are the verbs? You're the kind of person who listens to their intuition, you're the kind of person who doesn't ignore red flags, you're the kind of person who isn't afraid to ask awkward questions, you're the kind of person who respects their standards and boundaries?

Verbs. Verbs, my friend! They're the great equalizer in life. You can sit and write all the ways you want to feel, you can map out all your goals, you can have a five-year plan and a vision board and that's great... please do that. But at a certain point, those things need to become action. The best way to ingrain that in your mind is to be the kind of person who....

"I'm the kind of person who..." Then look at those things, those verbs, those actions. Are you doing them? No? That's OK, but now you know what to do.

You don't need to get lost in the abyss of overthinking because now when you're not feeling confident, happy, or successful, or you're not in a healthy relationship... you don't need to doubt yourself and feel like you're lacking. You simply know you just need to carry through with the things you say you need to do. You need to be the kind of person who...

That's much simpler, don't you think? That's much simpler than comparing yourself, beating yourself up, or nitpicking yourself. You just do what you say you're gonna do. Become the person you say you are. That's the kind of person who...

That person and the things that person does are always under your control, and whether they give you the outcome you want today... you'll always be on the right track if you carry through with those things.

The universe rewards people who are consistent with action. It rewards people who do those things no matter what and who do them even when they don't want to, even when they'd rather not, and when it's awkward or uncomfortable.

That's consistency, boldness, and a willingness to just do them. That is how you become those things you want to be - happy, successful, in love, etc.

You're the kind of person who...

CHAPTER EIGHTEEN

You Vs. the World

****

The world needs YOUR magic. The world needs creative, kind souls who aren't afraid to be awkward, extra, clueless, or "too much."

The world needs more people who live their lives with fearlessness, passion, and pizazz, who speak up, live, dream, chase curiosity, make mistakes, and who grab the aux cord to put on the song they want to hear in life.

The world needs YOU. The unfiltered version of YOU. The world needs you when you're at a '12' and everyone else is at a '2.'

Part 1. How You See the World

What do you think is the most important decision you'll make in your life? You might say it's the industry you decide to work in - medicine, business, art, music, construction, etc. You might say it's when and who you decide to marry. Or where you decide to live - urban, suburban, rural, etc. Or when/if you rent or buy a home or when/if you buy a car. Or if you decide to have kids, when, and how many. Or how you invest your money.

Those are important life decisions, and they undoubtedly have a material impact on your life. But I think there's one singular decision you'll make that has an even larger impact in your life. It's a decision of mindset, but it has just as much tangible impact as those practical decisions.

The question is, "Is the world for you or against you?"

The answer to that question dictates a lot of the happiness and fulfillment you'll create for yourself in your life.

Is the world for you or against you?

This question and what follows is predicated on the fact that the assumptions you make about yourself and the world around you create your reality. Your assumptions create reality.

What is an assumption? It's something you believe to be true without evidence to prove it. When you assume something to be true, you accept it as fact, and it influences the decisions you make or don't make. If you assume your friends are secretly talking badly about you behind your back, you're going to grow animosity and resentment against them - that's without evidence that they really are.

If you assume that 10/10 is out of your league, you're likely not going to shoot your shot - that's without any evidence that they're out of your league.

If you assume your dream job would never hire YOU, you're probably not going to apply - that's without any evidence that they wouldn't give you a chance. If you assume you're unlovable, ugly, lame, or weird, you're going to lower your standards - that's without any evidence that you need to.

There's nothing earth-shattering about this idea, and in fact, so much of what we do in the world of self-care is designed to combat those assumptions. I wrote this book to remind you of your worth, to help you find your heart and soul, to embrace your boldness, and to combat the negative assumptions your overthinking wants you to make.

Consider some of the assumptions you've made about the world around you. Is everyone and everything out to get you? Is the world against you? Does failure mean they won and you lost? Is rejection guaranteed in your life? Are people inherently mean, hurtful, and selfish? Or do you assume the opposite? No matter what happens in your life - decisions, failures, flops, and failed relationships - it's all conspiring to move you in a more redeeming direction? Are there good people and rewarding experiences available to you?

That's THE choice you have to make. It's the ultimate assumption in life.

How do you decide who you date, who you marry, where you work, what you do, and the risks you're willing to take or not take? Those are based 100% on the assumptions you make.

If the world is against you, what would that mean? It'd mean you're threatened by the people around you. You believe that both you and they can't succeed at the same time.

If someone is "better" than you in some way - better looking, smarter, more senior, etc. - they're going to succeed and you're not. And so, you give up easily.

If the world is against you, you compare yourself a lot and you judge yourself unfairly. You think everyone has it together and you don't. You're lost. And do lost people have confidence in their actions? Not really. You view everything in a cynical way. You think everyone else gets lucky and you don't. You think that if you're dating someone, they'll leave you as soon as they find someone better.

If the world is against you, you're expecting the worst to happen. You're expecting failure, heartbreak, or frustration. You're expecting to be lost, stuck, or alone. That's not to say that will come true just because you believe it, but you have to agree that those assumptions dictate your actions in some way, right?

You don't apply for your dream job. You accept what you have. You don't shoot your shot. You take whatever love is available to you. You don't practice what you love because it's silly and there's so many more talented people doing it.

But what if you believed the opposite? What if you made the choice to believe the world is FOR YOU? Well, that'd certainly change things. It doesn't make you reckless or delusional, but it means you have confidence in the direction your life takes no matter the Ws or Ls in the immediate.

It means you don't accept any ordinary love because you believe you deserve more. It means you don't take the first job you can because you believe you're capable of more. It means you love yourself and you expect the same of others. It means you believe in the power of effort and trying again and again and again.

You shoot your shot, you apply for that job, you start that business, or you make that investment. You believe in your ability to either succeed or rebound if you don't succeed.

THAT is the difference between an active life and a passive life. Wouldn't you say that's an important decision to make in your life?

Some of your life's best days haven't happened yet.

Is life for you or against you? If life is for you, that means that whatever you're going through will pass. That means you'll get another shot. That means you have the ability to try again. That means you shouldn't give up. That means you shouldn't hang it up and accept "good enough."

If life is for you, that means you might not know what tomorrow will bring, and even if today, yesterday, and the day before have been crappy, you have another day tomorrow to try again. That means that "100 assumption" is right around the corner. That means you get a second chance. If life is for you, that means you're committed to coming out stronger. A bad day doesn't mean a bad life. Starting over is OK because every time you do, you come out stronger, smarter, and more attractive.

That is THE assumption you can make about yourself and the world around you, and it dictates your actions. It dictates the many smaller decisions you'll make in your life.

It dictates what you accept or if you'll settle. It dictates the standards you set for yourself. It dictates your aspirations and dreams - how big are they? It dictates your expectations of others - do you demand from them the self-love you deserve? It dictates what you do and what you ask for - both of yourself and others.

Is the world for you or against you?

Part 2. There Are No Coincidences

If you believe life is FOR you, then it follows that there are no coincidences in life.

That means that when something happens or doesn't happen, when you're thrown a curveball, when you fail, when something completely out of left field happens, when the opposite of what you wanted happens… you can either chalk it up as a failure, a flop, and a reflection that you're not ready, you're not worthy, you're a big ol dummy, life is random and meaningless… OR you can simply say, "There are no coincidences in life." You can say, "This has to mean something. This has to be the new right way. This has to be a new path, a better path, or a different path that leads to something more redeeming."

What is a coincidence? According to the dictionary, a coincidence is "an accidental or remarkable occurrence of events or ideas at the same time, suggesting but lacking a causal relationship." It is the appearance of a meaningful connection when there really is none.

Sorry, Merriam Webster, but I'm saying that word does NOT exist. There are no coincidences. Everything IS connected in some way. There is no turn of events so arbitrary or so random to have no connection to a larger, different, or better path. There are no coincidences. Everything is connected, and in place of randomness and coincidence is faith.

There is nothing in life that is not connected.

I believe that a change in a game plan means a revised game plan, and no matter what happens, it's going to lead to what's meant to be. I believe we're always heading in a direction we're meant to be heading in.

When things happen - good, bad, unexpected - they are leading us there, and when that's the case, how could anything be a coincidence?

That's an event where there is ZERO connection to a larger purpose? I don't think that's possible. Everything is connected in some way.

Is it a coincidence that your relationship with someone ended, but then you ended up finding yourself and your standards in the process? Nope. Is it a coincidence that losing your job in a dramatic fashion led to a year off and you finding your passion? Nope. Is it a coincidence that embarrassing yourself in front of strangers led you to find your confidence? Nope.

Something in your past or present is inevitably going to lead to something redeeming in the future. And therefore, nothing is a coincidence. Nothing is disconnected. Nothing is completely random.

The challenge, of course, is that we rarely see the last part of those phrases until much later - finding your standards, finding yourself, your confidence, your passion, or your soulmate. In the moment, it's just a relationship that ended, a job lost, feeling anxious, or feeling down.

But those types of experiences inevitably lead you to find something about yourself. They inevitably lead you to another relationship, another job, or another purpose. And those inevitably lead to bigger, better, different, or more compassionate for YOU.

How can that journey be a coincidence? How can anything be random? How can anything not come to serve you in some way? How can something happen in life that is completely disconnected from your larger life path?

There are NO coincidences in life...
just cosmic signs you're on the right path.

I understand that this thinking really only works if you believe you deserve good things in life. This really only works if you believe that life is happening for you, not to you.

This really only works if you choose to believe that one door closed is another open.

I believe in the power of mindfulness in the most practical way possible. So, when it comes to an outlook on life, which of the following feels better? Thinking that everything is random, nothing is connected, and you're just lost at sea? OR thinking that whatever happens happens, but there are no coincidences, so it's 100% leading you somewhere redeeming, better, or different? Which feels better?

When you believe that life is random, one door shut is one door shut, you're just a sucker and life is happening to you- not for you... how does that make you feel? Anxious? Pessimistic? Frustrated? Lost. How do you feel when you suspend your cynicism and believe there are no coincidences - you're always being guided to something more redeeming? How do you feel? Hopeful? Optimistic? At peace?

I think life gets better when you realize that, yes of course, we can't always believe this, and yes anxiety and depression are very real... BUT when given the choice, how do you WANT to feel?

I'm sure you want to feel at peace and hopeful, right? Then try to make this a mantra of yours: There are no coincidences.

Mantras are powerful when you repeat them, when you believe them, and when you use them as the lens through which you view your life.

Choose what feels good for your soul. Choose what calms you. Choose what makes you hopeful. Choose it for the very reason that it feels much better in your heart and your body to believe in hope.

But also choose it because the more you believe something and the more you start viewing reality through that lens, the more you're going to find evidence that it's true.

The more you believe this, the more you'll start to look back, connect the dots, and realize that nothing in life didn't serve you in some way.

There wasn't any breakup that didn't lead you to something or someone better in some way. Or at minimum, there wasn't any breakup that didn't make your standards higher or your self-love more intact. There wasn't any turn of events with your friends, or job, or purpose in life that didn't lead you to a new path, a new opportunity, a new understanding of yourself, of what makes you happy, or what you're capable of. That is a choice and I hope you make it.

There are no coincidences.

Part 3. 20/20 Vision

I'm sure at some point - maybe even currently - you've found yourself in a cycle of negative mindsets, outcomes, or circumstances.

Maybe it's a long cycle of frustrating dating experiences - ghosted, "right person, wrong time," bad cringey first date after bad cringey first date, or repeated wasted time and energy on the wrong people. Maybe it's a pattern of feeling lost in your life - feeling that you're just going through the motions and you aren't finding fulfillment in anything you do. Maybe it's a pattern of low self-esteem - you feel that you're the world's unluckiest person, you're falling behind, and if anything can go wrong, it will. Maybe it's a pattern of anxiety - a long period of ambiguous stress in your life and you can't quite identify what it is, but it's this ever-present sense of gloom and doom.

How do you break free of these toxic patterns? Make a choice that a pattern does not define you.

A pattern does not define WHO you are.

A pattern defines what you've experienced.

A pattern is simply a series of events and that's that. Yes, it might be frustrating when it persists for a long period of time. Yes, it might really suck. Yes, it might really be the opposite of what you deserve or want. But let's see a pattern for what it is. It's a series of events.

We need to challenge how we see patterns. We tend to see a pattern as evidence of who we are. We see a pattern as proof of a flaw, an insecurity, or lack of worth. We look for evidence to support those assumptions, and a pattern over time leads us to assume we'll never break free, and we're not worthy of different or better. And so we do this very human thing where we find supporting evidence of that fact through the pattern itself.

Six bad dates in a row? Two failed long-term relationships in a row? Ghosted twice in a row? Two years without a promotion? Evidence. We see those experiences as evidence and we LEARN through them that we're not worthy of more, better, different, commitment, intention, etc.

Friends didn't text you to come out with them? Don't like the way you look in the mirror at the gym? Flopped that presentation at work? We see those experiences as evidence, and then we LEARN through them that we're not confident, we're not fun to be around, or we're not meant to be successful.

In reality, those experiences don't define WHO we are - they're just what we've experienced. But when left unchecked, we allow those experiences to teach us our identities. That's truly a self-taught curriculum. When we're in a pattern, it's no shock that we come to identify with it, and then that the pattern continues - all because we don't create a way out and we don't create a boundary between experiences and our identity. We close our eyes to the fact that a pattern is a pattern until it's not a pattern anymore. That sounds stupidly simple, doesn't it? But it's true.

A pattern is a pattern until it's not a pattern anymore.

Unfortunately, that's the way life is sometimes. A series of events or a pattern of frustrating outcomes is only that way until it's not anymore. It's only that way until you hit date one with that person who is right for you. It's only that way until you nail that presentation at work and get your mojo back. It's only that way until you find a new friend group, put in place a new boundary, finally speak up, etc.

When I'm in the midst of a bad pattern, I like to think of myself as being at a fork in a road. It goes left and it goes right. Left is, "I'm going to continue on this course because all the evidence suggests and has taught me that this is who I am."

But right is, "I will no longer look to my past experiences as proof that this is who I am." Right is a blank slate. Right is day one. That's a new day with new experiences where I say to myself, "If I come across those same patterns again on this day, so be it, but I will not allow it to teach me who I am. It's just an experience."

Can you look at the patterns in your life in this way? Can you say, "It's literally just an experience. I will not allow it to convince me that I'm unworthy of something. I will not allow a pattern of experiences to become a pattern of emotional assumptions. I will not allow a frustrating pattern of bad dates, bad days at work, or bad days in general become an assumption of insecurity, lack of worth, or lower standards.

Each day is a fork in the road. Left is allowing that pattern to become who you are, and right is a new day. You can choose left. "Today is another day in this pattern because this is who I am. My experiences are who I am." Or you can choose right. "Today is a new day. Yesterday's experiences are yesterday's experiences. I am not them."

It's a choice to stop looking for proof of the negative assumptions we make in life. Stop looking for proof that you're insecure, that you're unworthy, or that you're falling behind. A pattern will always support that notion, but the key to breaking free of it is to decide that you teach yourself what you choose.

Are you looking for proof that you're falling behind? No problem. Here's exhibit A, B, and C.

OR are you looking for proof that you're on the right track? Well, that lies on the other side of the pattern because YOU decide it does.

What evidence are you looking for?

If you're stuck in a cycle right now, what would happen if you stopped looking for evidence to support that pattern and instead looked for evidence that you're about to break through it?

What if you stopped seeing the people who rejected or ghosted you as proof that you're unworthy of commitment, and instead, you laughed at those people for having missed out on greatness? What if you chose the right fork and said, "That's their loss, and today, I know what kind of behavior to avoid, I have a stronger standard and more firm boundary?"

What if you stopped seeing your own self-criticism as a reflection of facts, and instead, started to assume that people looking at you are admiring you? You chose the right fork and you say people enjoyed your presentation at work, and that person on the street who looked at you was admiring you, not laughing at you? What if you stopped looking for proof of identity through a negative pattern, and instead, looked for evidence that you're breaking free?

Give yourself the gift of being at a fork in the road and choosing the right fork.

A pattern is only a pattern until it's not anymore.

Part 4. Strength in Loneliness

Contrary to how we'd prefer it to be, life is not supposed to always make sense. Life is supposed to be confusing. Life is supposed to take us by surprise. Life is supposed to be a rollercoaster. You find peace when you decide to see confusion as a sign you're moving toward what you deserve instead of away from it.

Life, growth, and progress are not part of a linear journey. It's not a straight line to what you want - it's up and down and down and up again. To say something like, "I'm not where I'm supposed to be" isn't fair to you because life has no timeline or blueprint to support that.

What do you mean "where you're supposed to be?" Where exactly are you supposed to be? What does that even mean? How can you possibly know that until you're there?

The purpose of life is to explore as many directions as possible and to help you examine whether it's right or wrong for you... and then push you in a new direction. Rinse. And repeat. So, it's necessary that things change. It's necessary that things are confusing at times. It's necessary that things don't work out how you wanted them to. To think that life is this thing where you make up your mind about what you want and who you're supposed to be, and then you just chip away at it and voila, you wake up and you're all those things... that's not fair to you, because each of those things is going to change as you grow.

Life is supposed to be confusing because confusion is what inspires change. Life is supposed to be frustrating because frustration inspires change. Frankly, life is supposed to hurt a bit because it changes you.

I think we need to drop this idea that life is either good or bad, you're either who you're supposed to be or you're not, or you're where you're supposed to be or you're not.

Life is all about the "in-between" days - the frustrating times, the times you feel lost, confused, uncertain, or unsure.

You can see a feeling of being lost as one that you're literally that - wandering without purpose or falling behind - OR that life is pushing you in a direction that serves you. Which do you choose?

To think you need it all figured out today and have it all accomplished today... is unrealistic. To think you're either who you need to be or you're not... that's unrealistic. Give yourself the gift of time. Give yourself the gift of embracing change over time.

Just ask any of the fine people I've listed here that have proven this.

Jeff Bezos didn't start Amazon until he was 31.

Terry Crews thought he wanted to be a professional football player and played in the NFL for four seasons. He spent all of his early life working toward that goal until making a big change to start acting when he was 32.

Vera Wang was a figure skater and a journalist for 39 years! She only started fashion when she was 40!

Sarah Blakely didn't start Spanx until she was 30, and before that, she was selling random goods door to door.

Life can take a long time to point you in the direction of what you're meant to be doing. It can take a long time to say, "THIS is why you're on earth" or, "THIS is where you're supposed to be."

To think you need to not only know that when you're 23 or even 30 and also HAVE it then is just absurd. It's not fair to you, and it detracts from the joy of life - which is the ride. It's the in-between days.

We have to drop our guards and realize that maybe life is supposed to be confusing at times. Maybe it's supposed to throw us for a loop from time to time? Maybe it's supposed to surprise us, frustrate us, make us angry, or even hurt us? Maybe it's through that process we finally figure out what we're supposed to do?

For each one of those A list names I listed, there are thousands of ordinary people like you and me who have beautiful stories of embracing change. Those are stories of people who turned 26 only to realize a new purpose, who turned 40 only to realize their worth in a relationship, or who turned 60 only to realize their creative side. What a beautiful journey life is… if we see it that way.

Life becomes peaceful when you see feeling lost as a positive sign. Life becomes peaceful when you feel uneasy and unsettled, but see it as a sign that you're being guided TOWARD what you want instead of AWAY from it. But let's be real, that process can be lonely. 2019 loneliness statistics show that 61% of adults reported feeling lonely. [1] Feeling lonely sucks. It's on par with a breakup, heartbreak, and loss in life. Sometimes we underestimate just how emotionally draining it is to be lonely and how, if we feel lonely for extended periods of time, it can lead to life-changing negative mentalities.

We've all felt literally alone in life - a time where we had fewer friends than we used to or a stage where we kept striking out in our dating lives … and there you are literally, physically, literally alone and lonely. But there's a deeper loneliness that's more a state of mind.

It's where you struggle to find connection to anything of substance. You struggle to find connection to people, your job, your purpose, or things that interest you - hobbies, entertainment, etc.

You feel alone in the world. You feel like you're the only person feeling that way. You feel like no one gets you. You feel like no one understands you - inside and out. You feel that YOU don't even understand you.

Loneliness is one of those topics where the quick and easy advice is: "It's OK to feel lonely because everyone feels lonely. You're not alone."

I suppose hearing that does make me feel a bit better. It gives a sense of universality to the human experience and helps us recognize that it's part of the process. But it doesn't stop the fact that feeling lonely is very draining and can cause you to doubt yourself, your worth, your passion, and your self-esteem.

So, first things first, realize you're not alone. Feel the loneliness. If you're lonely, feel lonely. Don't ignore it. Don't fight it. You can't heal what you refuse to feel. You can't improve what you refuse to address. But let's shift into a higher gear. Put your seatbelt on please. Here's what I've realized about feeling lonely as you embrace getting out of the gray in life:

I don't like patronizing self-help advice or any advice that isn't substantiated by a logical WHY. I'm not a fan of blanket statements like, "You deserve the best, you deserve to be loved"... well, yes of course! But why? Tell me why, and I'll 100% agree with you every time.

In the case of feeling lonely, what has really worked for me is realizing WHY I feel lonely. Once you realize why you feel lonely, it flips a switch from passive loneliness to active loneliness. That's from a defeated mentality to a fighter mentality.

I've realized that in life, it truthfully is easy to fill your head, your heart, and your calendar with things and people you're "supposed" to like.

It's easy to go on a date. It's easy to go on a second date. It's easy to go to happy hour. It's easy to watch *Netflix*. It's easy to get a dog. It's easy to get a new outfit. It's easy to play Fantasy Football. Those are easy things to do and acquire. I think there's a standard list of things you're supposed to do, get, and be happy with in life. And those things are supposed to be the antidote to feeling lonely because they provide the satisfaction and community you're looking for - or at least that you're supposed to be looking for. The average person finds connection to those things.

But I've found that the connection people make to those things is rarely their first choice, rarely their highest standard, or rarely aligned with their most compassionate WHY. It's amazing how easily we re-adjust our expectations for ourselves in life. It's amazing how quickly we lower the bar because we're tired, because we're impatient... or because we're lonely.

I vividly remember working a sales job when I was 27, and I was really lonely at the time - personally and creatively. I struggled to find connection to the work, I struggled to find connection to the people. I remember moments where I said to myself, "Maybe this is as good as it gets? Maybe I should calm down, take the money, adjust, and just be happy with this. Why am I so hungry for more?"

I also remember when I was 28 dating a woman but feeling so lonely in the relationship. Intuitively I knew we didn't have the compatibility I wanted, and I remember that little conversation in my head... "Well, she's hot, she's nice, she provides, and is there for me... maybe I just need to adjust?"

I remember those internal conversations so vividly - they were a response to feeling lonely. And I *almost* accepted them. I *almost* adjusted my expectations, my standards, and my vision to avoid feeling lonely.

It was all too easy to respond to loneliness by lowering the bar for myself. And ya know what? If I had done those things - if I had just said, "Case, shut up, it's a good job, people would kill for this. Case, relax she's good enough," - I would have realistically felt less lonely. It would've worked! It would've been the antidote to loneliness in the immediate. I could've very easily brainwashed myself into removing that feeling of loneliness. But for one reason or another, I didn't.

My point is, it's extremely easy to adjust your expectations for yourself. It's very easy to fill your life with things you're supposed to like and things you're supposed to connect with… and call it a day. It's very easy to respond to loneliness by lowering the bar. As humans, we are hardwired for self-preservation. We will do anything to protect ourselves physically, and we will do anything to protect ourselves emotionally. We do it subconsciously all the time without fully realizing it.

But let's realize WHY we feel lonely - we feel lonely because we have high standards that demand connection with the world around us, the people around us, and the work we do. And when we struggle to find that connection, we feel lonely.

A lot of people respond to that by lowering their threshold for that connection and downgrading the standard they have for themselves. It doesn't make them bad people, it's just the easy choice. And sometimes it's not even a choice, it's simple self-perseveration. If we're not careful, we slowly adjust until we accept that low connection as good enough for us.

"I don't really connect with those people, but it's better than being alone, so I'll be happy with it."

"I feel alone in this relationship, but he or she looks good on paper, so be it."

"I feel completely creatively drained at my job, but it's a job and I keep getting promoted, so I'll be happy."

"No one shares my interests and hobbies, so I guess I'll enjoy fantasy football, brunch, yoga, etc."

The way I've grown to see loneliness is that it is a response to your search for connection. You feel lonely when you haven't found the things, the people, the job, or the hobbies that make you feel connected. And so inherently, loneliness is a response to honesty. Loneliness is a response to your honest standards. Loneliness is a response to the honest expectations you have for yourself. And even though it hurts, I look at loneliness as the last remaining proof of your essence.

I'm not just saying this to come up with a redeeming story out of thin air or rationalize a negative feeling. I say this in the face of realizing just how easy it is to lose yourself in life. It's so easy to adopt other peoples' truths and checklists and timelines as your own. And so when I feel lonely, I see it as a strength. Because when you feel lonely and your response is NOT to lower the bar, that means you're not letting loneliness win. It means you're respecting your search for connection and you're not willing to adjust your standard to find it and get rid of that loneliness. It means you're respecting your intuition, your old soul nature, and the things that light up your eyes.

Loneliness is proof that your innate search for connection is intact.

That's a quote from PhD, Harvard-trained sociologist, and *New York Times* bestselling author, Martha Beck. And it's so true!

"Loneliness is proof that your innate search for connection is intact."[2]

To feel lonely, to feel a sense of longing for connection but to not have it, to yearn for passion and purpose and to be frustrated because you haven't found it... it's a sign that your search is still intact.

It's a sign you're still looking. It's a sign you haven't lowered your expectations for yourself. It's a sign you still believe in what you want and what you deserve.

How is that not a strength? How is that not redeeming in some way? It might not make you feel any less lonely in the immediate, but doesn't that fill your sails with a bit of wind? Doesn't it give you a small semblance of pride?

You had a choice and you're respecting the more difficult one. You're still searching. You haven't given up. You still believe in what you deserve.

You can respond to loneliness, like a lot of people do, by calling off the search, adjusting your standards and your expectations, and brainwashing yourself into a life that avoids the pain of that search. OR you can stand your ground and embrace it. You can keep searching despite the loneliness. And you can do that because you'd rather find that connection and make it last than give up in the middle of the journey.

Look at you! You'd rather keep searching than call it off because the storm makes you uncomfortable. That's something to be immensely proud of. You're still searching for what you deserve in every area of life. You're striving to determine what matters to YOU despite pressure to conform and fit in. You have standards that dictate what values you hold yourself to and the kind of people you date or are friends with.

Those might make you feel ostracized or lonely at times, but the fact you feel that way means you're still searching. You haven't given up. You haven't watered yourself down. You haven't accepted simply living in the gray of life.

Here is your new intention:

**For my next chapter, I'm doing more of
what makes my soul happy and at peace...
even if I have to do it alone.**

So, why do you feel lonely? It's NOT because of the reasons we as humans love to resort to and then respond to by lowering the bar - it's NOT because YOU can't connect with others. It's NOT because you're weird. It's NOT because you're awkward. It's NOT because of any inherent personal trait or what you deem is a flaw.

It's because you're still searching for the connection YOU deserve. End of story. And the feeling of loneliness is the side effect of searching. You're moving in the right direction. You're moving in the direction of living the life you deserve and finding the connection you deserve.

It's bold of you to know loneliness isn't a sign of lack of worth; it's a sign you're on the right track.

Part 5. That's Bold of You

It's time to be bold. But WHY?

This entire book has been an inquisition into the WHYs in your life. Why do you feel compelled to do certain things or act a certain way? Why do you tend to step back when you really want to step forward? Why do you accept timelines, expectations, and adjectives that don't apply to you? Why why why? I hope you feel a bit more honest and empowered right now to start a new chapter where you embrace what feels real to you - in the face of pressure to conform and labels that don't describe the real you.

I'll leave you with one more WHY. Why should you act boldly in all areas of your life?

You should be bold for the simple reason you know what it's like to NOT be bold. You have contrast in your life from experiences where you let labels, pressure, and conditioning talk you out of living as your most vibrant and real self. You've let other people's definitions become your own. You've let other people's opinions of you become your own. You've been hurt, watered down, and disappointed. That is the human experience, and like so many, you've experienced all of its varieties.

But here you are still standing with those chapters in the rear-view mirror. Here you are with a new definition of YOU - one that is defined by your ability to be bold and forgive yourself for acting otherwise. You've forgiven the version of yourself who was okay with living in the gray.

That's the version of yourself who held onto people who didn't hold onto you, who didn't ask for more when you knew you deserved it, who kept looking for love in the same places you lost it, who tried to be the person other people wanted you to be, who only gave love and never saved any for yourself, who blamed yourself when someone didn't know how to love you, and who thought a high standard would scare off the right person.

You've lived through those chapters, and here you are defined by your ability to be bold. That's bold enough to be imperfect…

Bold enough to love. Bold enough to start over. Bold enough to forgive yourself. Bold enough to speak and act freely.

Why should you be bold? Because you know what it's like to tiptoe around people, trying to be everyone's cup of tea, and where "sorry" is the most common word out of your mouth. You know what it's like to change your wants, needs, or behavior to make sure everyone around you is comfortable. You know what it's like to drop your boundaries to practically nothing. You know what it's like to succumb to advice, timelines, or definitions that are "realistic."

You know what it's like to make yourself small in the face of your big goals and aspirations. You know what it's like to stick it out in relationships that no longer serve you. You know what it's like to hide truths about yourself - your past, your hurt, or your pain. You know what it's like to sugarcoat your words and what you really want to say. You know what it's like to let other people have the spotlight. You know what it's like to take a step back when everything inside of you wants you to step forward.

That is your WHY. That is the source of your real, unforced, and authentic boldness.

You know what it's like to NOT be bold. You know what it's like to live in the gray of life, and now after 18 chapters of peeling back the layers, I hope you're empowered to do the opposite.

Your time spent in the gray of life has been pointing you toward your real self, not away from it.

You know the value of your words, your energy, your presence, and your aspirations. You've seen the opposite. You've lived in that space for long enough, and now it's time to be bold.

It's time to shine your light, speak your mind, and embrace your own labels of being "too much." It's time to please yourself for once and create a vision for life that is YOURs and yours alone. It's time to replace conformity with curiosity, expectations with truth, and judgment with forgiveness.

If you're reading this, you have a beautiful heart, kind energy, a powerful voice, passion, and pizazz for a reason. You're exactly who you're supposed to be.

Being bold doesn't mean you're full of yourself. It doesn't mean you're the loudest person in the room. It doesn't mean you're obnoxious or you make other people feel uncomfortable. It doesn't mean you're perfect.

It simply means you embrace the "beautiful mess" of your life in everything you do. You embrace the imperfection of your life's journey and you prioritize radical honesty above everything else and your actions follow.

It means you're exactly who you're supposed to be.

Want more?

Listen to *New Mindset, Who Dis?*
wherever you listen to podcasts.

Research References

Introduction
[1] Pazzanese, Christina. *"Portman: I, Too, Battled Self-doubt."* Harvard Gazette, 19 Mar. 2019, news.harvard.edu/gazette/story/2015/05/portman-i-too-battled-self-doubt.

Chapter One
[1] *"Japanese Wabi-Sabi Design."* Envato, 29 Oct. 2020, www.envato.com/blog/japanese-art-wabi-sabi.

[2] Itani, Omar. *"5 Teachings From the Japanese Wabi-Sabi Philosophy That Can Drastically Improve Your Life."* OMAR ITANI, 24 Apr. 2021, www.omaritani.com/blog/wabi-sabi-philosophy-teachings.

[3] Ayuda, Tiffany. *"How The Japanese Art of Kintsugi Can Help You Deal With Stressful Situations."* NBC News, 28 Apr. 2018, www.nbcnews.com/better/health/how-japanese-art-technique-kintsugi-can-help-you-be-more-ncna866471.

[4] Kempton, Beth. *Wabi Sabi: Japanese Wisdom for a Perfectly Imperfect Life.* Illustrated, Harper Design, 2018.

[5] Leonard Koren. *Contemporary Wabi-Sabi Style.* Artpower International, 2022. Page 59.

[6] Leonard Koren. *Contemporary Wabi-Sabi Style.* Artpower International, 2022. Page 40.

Chapter Two
[1] Kerr, Natalie, MD. *The Benefits of Letting Yourself Be Vulnerable,* www.psychologytoday.com/us/blog/social-influence/202110/the-benefits-letting-yourself-be-vulnerable.

[2], [3], [4] Bruk, A., Scholl, S. G., & Bless, H. (2018). *Beautiful mess effect: Self–other differences in evaluation of showing vulnerability. Journal of Personality and Social Psychology,* 115(2), 192–205. https://doi.org/10.1037/pspa0000120

Chapter Four

[1] Johnson, R. Skip. *"Escaping Conflict and the Drama Triangle"*. 4 Jan. 2021, bpdfamily.com/content/karpman-drama-triangle

[2] Forrest, SW, Lynne (26 June 2008). "The Three Faces of Victim — An Overview of the Drama Triangle". https://www.lynneforrest.com/articles/2008/06/the-faces-of-victim/

[3], [4], [5], [6] Murdoch, B.Ed., Edna. "The Karpman Drama Triangle". Coaching Supervision Academy. https://web.archive.org/web/20150611084230/http://coachingsupervisionacademy.com/thought-leadership/the-karpman-drama-triangle/

Chapter Six

[1] Maryam Hasnaa On Twitter, 17 May 2020, twitter.com/maryamhasnaa/status/1262060804066566144.

[2] Sartori, Penny, and Kelly Walsh. *The Transformative Power of Near-Death Experiences: How the Messages of NDEs Can Positively Impact the World*. Watkins Publishing, 2017. PG 15

[3] Ever Present at the Getty (Getty Museum Programs) www.getty.edu/museum/programs/performances/ever_present.html.

Chapter Seven

[1] "Mimetic Theory | *What It Is - Mimetic Theory,* 12 Apr. 2020, mimetictheory.com/what-it-is-2.

[2] Palaver, Wolfgang. René Girard's Mimetic Theory. Michigan State UP, 2013.

[3] *"The Age of Anxiety? Birth Cohort Change in Anxiety and Neuroticism, 1952-1993,"* Jean M. Twenge, PhD, Case Western Reserve University; Journal of Personality and Social Psychology, Vol. 79, No. 6.

[4] Montesquieu, "the Spirit of Laws," Book IV. classicliberal.tripod.com/montesquieu/sol04.html.

Chapter Eight

[1], [2] *McLeod, S. A. (2018, Dec 28). Solomon Asch - Conformity Experiment.* Retrieved from https://www.simplypsychology.org/asch-conformity.html
[3], [4] Asch, S. E. (1956). *Studies of independence and conformity: I. A minority of one against a unanimous majority.* Psychological monographs: General and applied, 70(9), 1-70.

Chapter Nine

[1] Communications, Nyu Web. *New And Diverse Experiences Linked to Enhanced Happiness, New Study Shows.* www.nyu.edu/about/news-publications/news/2020/may/new-and-diverse-experiences-linked-to-enhanced-happiness--new-st.html.
[2] *"New And Diverse Experiences Linked to Enhanced Happiness, New Study Shows." NSF - National Science Foundation,* beta.nsf.gov/news/new-diverse-experiences-linked-enhanced-happiness.

Chapter Eleven

[1], [2], [3] *Cell Press. "When it comes to our brains, there's no such thing as normal." ScienceDaily. ScienceDaily, 20 February 2018.* www.sciencedaily.com/releases/2018/02/180220123129.htm

Chapter Twelve

[1] Smith, Oliver. *"Whether You're a Believer or Not, the Shinto Ritual of Waterfall Bathing Offers a Chance to Reset — and Immerse Yourself in the Spiritual Beauty of Japan's Mountains."* National Geographic, 16 Mar. 2021, www.nationalgeographic.co.uk/travel/2020/05/diving-into-misogi-the-ancient-japanese-ritual-of-waterfall-bathing.
[2] Bethea, Charles. *"Kyle Korver's Grind Activator."* The New Yorker, 15 May 2015, www.newyorker.com/sports/sporting-scene/kyle-korvers-grind-activator.
[3] Steindl-Rast, David. *"Want to Be Happy? Be Grateful."* TED Talks, 27 Nov. 2013, www.ted.com/talks/david_steindl_rast_want_to_be_happy_be_grateful?

[4] VFI / Alleged Quote. www.viktorfrankl.org/quote_stimulus.html.

Chapter Fourteen
[1] Genovese, Maddalena. *"Dear Maddi: Social Comparison and Studying Enough."* Faculty of Science, 6 Oct. 2021, www.ualberta.ca/science/student-services/student-life-engagement/wellness-matters/dear-maddi/2021/october/dear-maddi-social-comparison.html.
[2] dictionaryofobscuresorrows. "Sonder." Tumblr, 22 July 2012, www.dictionaryofobscuresorrows.com/post/23536922667/sonder.

Chapter Sixteen
[1], [2] Oakley, David. *"Chasing the Rainbow: The Non-conscious Nature of Being."* Frontiers, 2017, www.frontiersin.org/articles/10.3389/fpsyg.2017.01924/full.
[3], [4] *"SF State Researcher Explores How Information Enters Our Brains."* SF State News, news.sfsu.edu/archive/news-story/sf-state-researcher-explores-how-information-enters-our-brains.html

Chapter Seventeen
[1] "(Serious) What Is the Most Helpful Thing Your Therapist Has Ever Said to You?" Reddit, 15 Oct. 2020, www.reddit.com/r/AskReddit/comments/jbmpei/comment/g8ww5am/

Chapter Eighteen
[1] Rameer, Vanessa Mae. *"US Loneliness Statistics 2022: Are Americans Lonely?"* Science of People, 12 Oct. 2022, www.scienceofpeople.com/loneliness-statistics.
[2] Beck, Martha. *"When You Feel Lonely."* Martha Beck, 21 Jan. 2018, marthabeck.com/2012/11/when-you-feel-lonely